GOD Among Us
Inside the Mind of the Divine Masters

with great love!

Carol

GOD Among Us
Inside the Mind of the Divine Masters

Caroline Cory

OMnium Books

GOD Among Us: Inside the Mind of the Divine Masters

Copyright © 2005 by Caroline Cory

All rights reserved. This book may not be reproduced in whole or in part without the written permission of the publisher.

For more information about this book, please visit www.omniumfoundation.com
To contact the author, please e-mail author@omniumfoundation.com

13-digit ISBN: 978-0-9766116-1-5
10-digit ISBN: 0-9766116-1-9
Printed in the United States of America by:

Signature Book Printing, Inc.
www.sbpbooks.com

This text is dedicated to...

My Divine Father

Acknowledgements

*To the Assembly of 7 and 12, Antoine, my Divine Mother,
my Divine Brother Gabriel,
Mu, Edwar, Vyrgyle, and beloved John,
Thank you for being there for me.*

Contents

INTRODUCTION xi

Part I
1. A Story Begins 1
2. The Initiation 7

Part II
3. The Remembrance 39
4. The Original Home 67
5. The Original Spirit Family 81
6. The Agreement 101
7. The Mission 109

Part III
8. A Call for Action to All: Manifesting the Divine Plan on Earth 133
9. Practical Tools & Prayers:
   - Living a Perfected Spiritual Life 135
   - Managing your Thoughts and your Human Mind 139
   - Understanding your Emotions 145
   - Summoning the Cosmic Forces for Help 148

MY FAITH, MY TRUTH, MY CONCLUSION 155

GLOSSARY 157

Introduction

My journey began when I started to fully experience the meaning of "Ask and you shall receive". The simplicity of this statement can be quite deceiving and quite powerful at once. To my amazement, I began to ask, and all that I asked for, I received. I am not referring to material needs but rather those experiences of the mind and spirit, those that are called "miraculous" in this physical reality as we know it.

Those who have read my previous book, *The Visible and Invisible Worlds of GOD*, may know of my ability to communicate with the Creator-Source[1] or Source Energy[2]. Source Energy is the energy of the one universal Creator / Source of all beings and things, or that which we call the *All That Is*. It is experienced in the physical realms through the persons of the Divine Father[3] and the Divine Mother[4] who are the direct Creators of our species, this universe and the universes surrounding ours. I have created a diagram which shows the roadmap of this universal organization to help you visualize the process of reaching and communing with Source Energy from our earthly reality to the core of our creation. (See figure 1 on page xiii)

From this expanded perspective and understanding, I began to ask about the divine truths as they are experienced by those we call the *Sons of God*[5] and the *Divine Ascended Masters*[6] that walked this earth. I asked: "What would it be like to be in physical form and experience our true divine and infinite self? Who are those we call Gods

---

1 Creator-Source: First and Original Creator of all life, intelligent beings and things in existence.
2 Source Energy: Energy emanating from the Source of all creation.
3 Divine Father: Replica of the Creator-Source (expression aspect) and original creator of earth, its universe, all surrounding universes and intelligent life therein.
4 Divine Mother: Replica of the Creator-Source (spirit aspect) and original creator of earth, its universe, all surrounding universes and intelligent life therein.
5 Sons of God: Beings that embody the Divine Father / Divine Mother in material / human form.
6 Ascended Master: Beings in human form that have mastered the human condition.

and Masters and how do we become one? How can I be of service to humanity in a big way?"

As expected the answers came. What was unexpected was *the way* in which they came. Not only did I receive and understand these messages, I also began to truly experience the *mind and spirit* of these Masters along with many extraordinary and supernatural phenomena. My experiences ranged from accessing and listening in clearly on the collective human mind matrix[7], to manifesting actual documents such as non-existent symbols on the stock market index! I was so perplexed by some of the episodes I experienced along the way, that I had to be sure of my own sanity before speaking of such events to anyone I knew. However, with time, I understood that these incidents and bizarre events were meant to be shared, as they are part of the process of expanding the human mind and spirit. So, I wrote this book to share with you these incredible experiences in an attempt to convey that these Gods and Masters with highly evolved divine intelligence are but our own potential and destiny - if we simply ask.

For clarity, I divided the book in 3 parts. Part I describes my personal experiences as I merged with the consciousness of the Masters and began a mind training and re-programming process that the Masters undergo when they realize their own divinity and soul lineage while in the flesh. It is meant to help you prepare for the awakening of your own divinity or simply allow you to recognize similar experiences you may have had that seemed inexplicable or incoherent. Part II is the compilation of information and messages retrieved from communications between the Masters and the Divine Creator[8] regarding their nature, their original home, their pre-natal contract and earthly mission. Part III offers practical tools and prayers for your own self-realization and for the mastery of your human mind and spiritual enlightenment.

When I asked Source for guidance about this book, the answer was as follows: "This book is about the divine beings and masters as they walked on this earth. You are connected to the mind of these extraordinary beings as they lived their lives as humans on earth. You connect to their mind through a unique arrangement that allows you to retrieve information directly from their memory cells."

---

7   Human mind matrix: Frequency where all human minds and thoughts meet.
8   Divine Creator: Both the Divine Father and the Divine Mother combined.

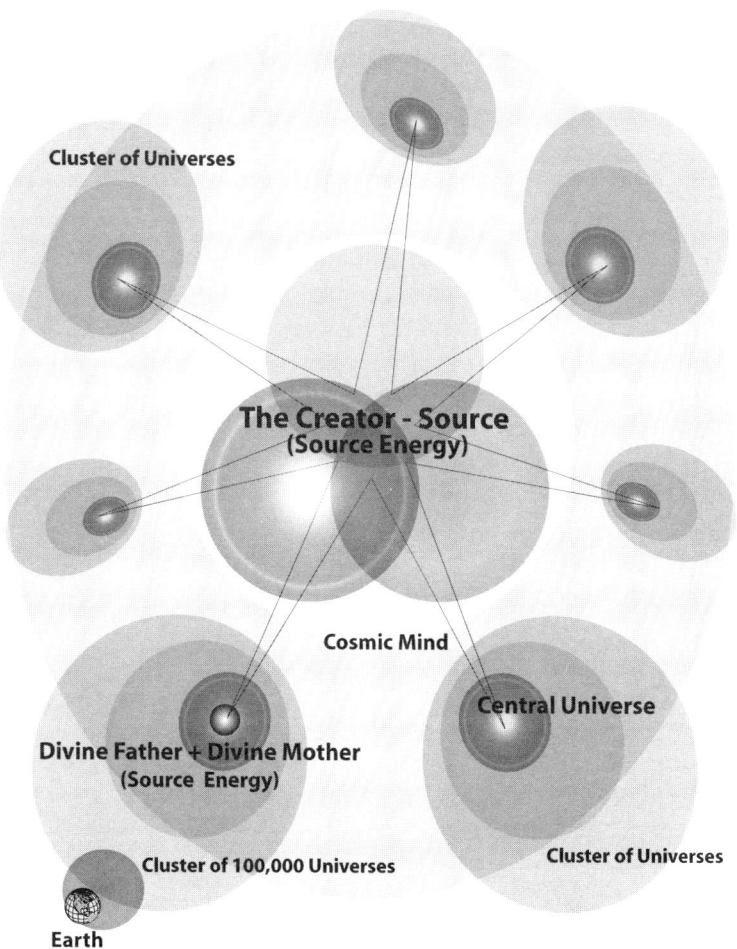

FIGURE 1: Source Energy, filtered through the Divine Father and the Divine Mother, is our direct link to the Creator-Source

With that, I have no doubt about the meaning and reason for this material. However, to insure clarity and purpose for the reader, I must add that, while the information herein may reflect the particulars of certain Masters, it is nonetheless applicable to *all* beings (human, evolutionary, celestial, divine etc…) as *an ultimate potential*, when they embody the human form.

So, as you read these pages, allow your mind to *open to the possibility* of your own inherent divinity and your guidance will bring forth that which is aligned with your higher good and unique purpose. More importantly, enjoy this journey and make no judgment. If this book managed to make it into your hands, it is purposely so. As always, love and blessings are encoded herein.

Part I

1
A Story Begins

What I am about to disclose in this chapter is the result of my blending with the minds of the Divine Masters that walked this earth. This merging happened spontaneously as I engaged in a simple meditation exercise. What ensued, however, were a series of extraordinary events that lasted over 14 months. These occurrences do not necessarily imply that all individuals merging with this higher consciousness or simply awakening to their divinity will encounter exactly similar circumstances. These accounts serve to show, not only what the Divine Masters undergo during their own awakening, but are also an example of a process that all humans must follow to achieve what we call "enlightenment". The particulars of the process itself, however, will differ from one individual to the next according to their own life contract.

◆ ◆ ◆

January 2000. This was the beginning of the strangest years of my life. While I consider myself sensitive and quite familiar with the spirit world, what happened to me during this period was beyond anything I could ever imagine or expect. Both worlds, the visible and invisible, had suddenly merged and made my existence utterly exquisite and miserable all at once.

My story began on a hot and breezy day in Florida. I was sitting quietly on my porch, appreciating the silence and beauty of nature, when I noticed that the red ant stings I had gotten on the beach earlier that afternoon had swollen and formed a huge bulge on my right thigh. As I stared at it apprehensively, I suddenly heard a voice saying: "Ask the lump to disappear. Ask the swelling to stop and disappear." Without questioning the reason or origin of the voice, I asked the malicious bulge to go away. To my astonishment, it began to shrink, and within seconds, it had vanished completely before my eyes! I was terrified. I ran inside and hid in the bedroom trying to contain my emotions and pounding heart. What had I done, and how could that be? Is it possible to simply ask and make such things happen instantaneously? To say the least, I was baffled and disturbed but quickly managed to dismiss the incident as a ploy of my own mind and imagination.

The voice, however, returned the next day. As I felt the urge to indulge in a soft ice cream treat, the voice suddenly interjected: "Ask your ice cream to taste salty… Ask it to taste salty." Without hesitation, I asked and it did! Upon command, the ice cream tasted sour, then bitter. This time, I was less disturbed by my achievement, even though I was still puzzled by the mysterious voice and certainly, the meaning of these peculiar experiences.

Later on, I watched my friend lay in pain from a lower back injury, when the voice once more spoke: "Ask to relieve his pain. All you have to do is *ask*." Curious about these odd happenings, I decided to attempt to help him somehow. I began placing my hand on his lower back area when he suddenly shrieked: "Stop!… You burned me!" His reaction startled me - to say the least - and as I stared incomprehensibly at the palm of my hand, I wondered: "How could I burn him when my hand is still 4 or 5 inches away from his body? What sort of energy could possibly emanate from my hand, penetrate his shirt and burn his skin?!"

I began a frantic search for the truth behind my little daily miracles. The more I searched, the more I realized that my "askings" or *thoughts* had created my experiences. I came to understand the dynamics of creating reality instantly using my own mind and not just my physical sensations but my outer reality as well - all of it. With time, and as these occurrences continued on a regular basis, I found that I was able to stop unbearable physical pain and alter negative emotions, such as anger or fear of any intensity, practically on the spot. All I had to do was focus and ask.

    I decided to experience more the process by which my thought *affected and created* my environment. That day, I was in a movie theatre where the temperature of the room felt uncomfortably cold. I decided to deliberately become comfortable without asking the attendant to turn up the temperature of the entire room. Seconds later, I began to experience the physical comfort I was looking for and realized that it was *my perception* and *my experience* of that environment that was altered. Regardless, I had deliberately manifested an immediate physical response that was advantageous to me and that was pretty incredible indeed. The more I focused my thoughts on what I wanted to manifest, the more it worked. I was no longer a victim of circumstances but the true creator of my own experience.

    At one point, I wondered how my mind could also be affecting people around me. If my thoughts affect my environment, to what extent, then, were my thoughts affecting individuals I was interacting with? Was I perhaps creating my reality at the expense of others? The very idea that I could remotely affect someone else's experience was very disconcerting to me. I was concerned that such a notion would not only imply a true violation of human free will, but also would be in contradiction with what I had discovered in the first place - that each individual creates his or her own experience. I came to the conclusion that if I were creating my own experience, well then, so is the rest of the world.

    Time went on, and I continued expanding my awareness to other areas of *conscious creation*. I began to dream specific dreams that I had consciously asked for. I realized that deliberate thoughts were my tools for creating any experience, in my physical life or other realities as well, such as my dreams and even past experiences. While I could not change the circumstances of a past event, I could alter my experience of it; thereby liberate myself from negative emotional blocks and mental patterns associated with that experience.

    The reason it is difficult for humans to see the obvious correlation between their thoughts and outer reality is due to the fact that thoughts are invisible - to humans, that is. Through my daily miracles, I, on the other hand, began to perceive my thoughts and others'. They appear as actual physical *energy clusters* that travel through space (and time) within a frequency range below or above the human perceptual spectrum, therefore remain invisible. These energy clusters are maneuvered by (spirit) beings that are in charge of such energetic manipulation and are transported by means of electromagnetic grids. Thought particles are infinitesimal and several hundred of them are equal to the size of one human atom or molecule. I, nonetheless, could actually see, sense and hear my thoughts travelling back and forth to other individuals or locations and I realized that this was precisely the process of telepathic communication. Little did I know, however, that it would come to work so effortlessly!

TELEPATHIC CONTACT ...

One evening, as I explored these theories of thought transfer through focused visualization, I suddenly felt a "force" connecting with me through my forehead. It felt like someone was drawing air out of my third eye[9] as if it pulled my thoughts into an invisible beam of some sort. I had established telepathic contact with someone! He calmly said: "My name is Mu. I live in South Africa and wish to communicate with you. Let me be clear. I am not of this world either. I can be in physical form in order to communicate with you. However, I can also become invisible at will. This is the future of humankind - a disease-free society, experienced in spirituality to a degree that is unimaginable to you now."

It took me a while to come to terms with this event and the other breakthroughs that continued manifesting in my life. I certainly was not ready to discuss them openly with anyone at the time as I was not sure if I was becoming strange or superhuman. While I was amazed at my growing psychic abilities, I could not help noticing how odd my experiences were, as they happened spontaneously, effortlessly, repeatedly and without warning.

---

9 Third eye: Intuitive sight. Corresponds to the area of the forehead between the eyes or what is referred to as the 6th Chakra.

In a relatively short period of time (3 or 4 months), I began to see and experience reality as multi-dimensional or multi-layered. While physical reality appears linear and chronological, I could cross over from one reality to the next, travel back and forth through the time / space continuum and consciously peak into my parallel lives. Not only could I hear the answers to my most intricate questions, but I could have actual exchanges, through my thoughts, with other portions of myself (my spirit self[10] and other particles of my being that exist in other physical incarnations) as well as other beings. While I was amazed at my exploits, my human mind still wondered if I wasn't fringing some sort of schizophrenic episodes or incurred a serious mental imbalance of the sorts.

Just as I began to sink into worry and confusion, the following extraordinary experience happened. I was calmly strolling along the beach when I suddenly saw a most powerful energy of utmost beauty appear before me in the form of a giant cloud. The tremendous love, beauty and brilliant light that emanated from this energy were overwhelming. I realized that this energy was *a being*. In fact, it was a being I knew well as it felt so familiar and comfortable, even though I was unable to discern its precise identity in that moment. Regardless of what or who it was, this being was of enormous magnitude as it felt as vast as the entire sky, as powerful as the strongest wind, as stunning as the most breathtaking scenery. Suddenly, all was well, in perfect balance and harmony. I was transported to a space of reality where there was no need, no dichotomy, no separation and no paradox. It was purely positive and divinely exquisite. In this space, I knew that I could access everything and anything I envisioned. In this instant, I could have answers to all my questions, achieve all the healing I wished for and materialize all that my heart desired.

My life was now simultaneously exhilarating and frightening. While I bathed in this divine reality that had suddenly opened to me, I also began to feel as if this world (earth) had not only stopped progressing but had, somehow, regressed in time. I felt as if I had just appeared from the "future" and that everything and everyone suddenly seemed dreary and dull to the point of making this reality unbearable to live in.

Meanwhile, the voice, which I eventually identified as *Antoine*, would intermittently emerge to recite interminable and absurd mes-

---

10   Spirit self: Outer most portion of the human energy field, also called higher self.

sages such as this one: "You are of God and God is the All That Is and the All That Is is God and God are here to heal this world because you are God and of God and not human..." What?! Not human? This remark sounded shocking in that moment as I felt "alien-like". However, the more I fought the idea, the more these recitations became louder and incessant.

Hmmm... I was now becoming very confused. About who I was, why I was here, my work, my career, others around me, everything! And who was Antoine anyway and what was he doing in my life at that particular juncture? I could now clearly perceive him even though he remained invisible to others. He appeared as a holographic figure of some sort but clear enough to distinguish his features and the details of his attire. He was a high priest as he wore a long robe that was royal blue with red and gold ornament. He was bald and appeared well proportioned but somewhat small. He was very funny, loving and brilliant in his way of directing my thoughts. We communicated telepathically mostly in English, sometimes in French as I am fluent in both. Either way, I heard him loud and clear, just like any conversation I would carry with another being in human form.

I felt that we were "family" somehow and later found out that a couple of his human manifestations had been as a high priest of Rennes-Le-Chateau[11] in the late 1700's and the Count of St. Germain in the 1500's. He said he was my *spirit father*[12] during many life aspects[13] but he was truly the representative and link to my *Divine Father in Heaven* as he was in charge of orchestrating my earthly awakenings and connecting me back to Him. However, regardless of my relationship with my dear guide, I was more concerned and occupied, at that time, with the peculiar feelings I was experiencing rather than retracing my genealogical lineage!

---

11   Rennes-Le-Chateau: Area in the south of France known for its mystical and sacred energy.
12   Spirit father: Father figure in spirit form.
13   Life aspects: What is recognized as human lifetimes.

2

The Initiation

Over another period of 3 or 4 months, Antoine persistently urged me to *do nothing*, to expect nothing. And so, I began to do nothing. But how do you really *do* nothing? I assumed I was creating mind space to allow more important things to happen. However, Antoine mentioned that this exercise was allowing the remembrance and healing of *all* my earthly existences, in order to proceed. All? How many could there be?

Ignoring my questioning and confusion, he initiated the excruciating exercise of digging up memories out of my other earthly existences[14]. I began to *remember* being physically tortured, abused, possessed, at the mercy of terrifying mental illnesses and accused of being an evil-doer - all of which I know did not happen in this lifetime! These experiences were a painful mental torture and I truly experienced them as *real* as if they happened to me at that very moment. There was nothing I could do to stop them and now, I was truly concerned I was at the verge of losing my mind.

The mental harassment and accusations persisted for weeks and months, which seemed like eternity. Finally, Antoine's empathy took over and he explained that it was because the Masters merge with the Divine Father, they will or must experience *all* human experiences, good or bad, as the Divine Father also experiences all human events. Oh, that's a relief! But now, my confusion was turning into real exasperation. My spirit friend insisted, however, that experienc-

---

14 Other earthly existences: parallel / past human life incarnations.

ing all human suffering would allow me to understand it. This did not mean the suffering of every single human being since the beginning of time but rather, all *possible* positive or negative experiences (such as violence or isolation) that any given being would incur within this physical reality and this human condition.

I have to admit that I had my share of human suffering - as we understand it – in this lifetime. My childhood was rather disconnected from what I would call real love. Growing up, I felt out of place among my peers and family members. I had several childhood illnesses and was in a tragic car crash at the age of 17 that left me temporarily paralyzed. This experience allowed me to cross over and return to the physical reality. It took months to recover from this dire physical and emotional trauma. I would think that is a fair amount of "human suffering" for one lifetime. However, there was more to experience. And the remainder – abuse, torture and violence - I experienced in my mind (as real events happening to me), for weeks at a time, under the guidance of beloved Antoine, that is. In each case, he would retrieve these memories and transmute them into beneficial energy instantaneously. It was as if he waived a magic wand at each surfacing trauma and spontaneously dissolved it into a puff of light and love energy. However, *during* the process, the mental suggestions he offered were just as powerful and painful as in a physical sense. And that was precisely the point – experience happens through the mind – but by the time I surfaced from this prolonged mental trial, I was truly exhausted!

Needless to say, continuous communication with spirit guides can also be quite confusing at first. While I could experience the presence of spirit beings, such as Antoine, I was quite uncomfortable carrying on a conversation with an invisible counterpart for a prolonged period of time, because I felt detached from this physical reality or felt that I functioned within it in an odd and unusual manner. Also, I found these exchanges difficult to sustain - for long periods of time - until I eventually acquired the necessary control of switching focus from one reality to another.

MORE SUPERNATURAL EXPERIENCES ...

Regardless of my feelings, my spontaneous and powerful spiritual experiences continued. That day, I wrote: "In the past few weeks, I have been having strange feelings of disappearance. I feel my body does not exist and that I am disappearing from this reality. I feel in an altered state as if blended with air. When I look at others or things around me, they appear to exist in a movie-like reality. I don't understand what they are doing or what they are about. I wonder if I have crossed over somehow as I can barely contain my spirit inside my body. It is as if *I am* the entire space and that this body is simply not mine."

I continued: "I see myself as a spirit floating in space between this planet earth and other parts of the Milky Way. There are large beams of light going through my being, connecting me to all points of the galaxy as if my physical body was a bridge sustaining the light passing through it. My physical head feels as if it were the entire planet. It *is* this earth! I notice that different points on my skull relate to various areas of this earth. It is a most strange yet delightful experience. I am one with earth, *I am* the earth!"

Later, I wrote more: "I am floating in space, this time in the outer universal band[15]. Each portion of my physical body blends with one part of the universe. My brain is the core or centre of the universe; my veins are the communication system between the worlds; my blood is the liquid of the oceans and rivers; my bones form the chemical make up of the planets; my neurological system is the electrical wiring of the different planes; my flesh is the surface upon which energy floats; my heart is the pulse, my voice is the sound, my energy is the light and my breath is what sustains life within this entire universe. *I am* this universe!"

While I bathed in this exquisite experience, I noticed electric energy sparkling from my eyes and face as I connected with Source or the universal centre. Powerful information travelled back and forth between this core of creation and my physical eyes, here in material form. It was a most intriguing yet delightful sensation. However, when I focused back on my earthly existence, my awareness changed: "I feel so disappointed when I observe what humans have

---

15   Universal band: Edge of the universe.

done to themselves, to each other and to this planet. I am saddened to see their anger and their hatred towards each other. I have nothing to do here. This is not the place for me. I simply want to leave..." During these moments, I think this *is* hell, a prison of the mind, the most limited aspect of all life. I am overwhelmed by a tremendous feeling of disappointment with this physical world. Nothing seems to matter other than my love for my Divine Creator, the Divine Father in Heaven."

However, my experience carried on: "I can see that something of massive importance is about to happen. Not on the scale of one or a few countries, but on a global, even galactic scale. I am very saddened by it as I realize this may be the end of many realities and many individuals at once. I see fear, chaos and panic on a colossal scale. There are weapons but the destruction also happens through mass electrical and electromagnetic clashes and everywhere, there are deaths and more deaths. I am deeply saddened by this vision."

"I can see a very dark and thick cloud of deadly smoke, and nothing beyond it. There is total void as if life, as we know it, will no longer be. I am deeply saddened to recognize that this time will come to pass. It is the time when all those who created these calamities at the expense of others or for their personal and egotistical aims, will perish and disintegrate. Soon, very soon, life on earth, as we know it, will never be the same."

As I finished my thought, I felt my body's protective shield[16] suddenly strip off, and I found myself in the presence of a terrible and evil force. This powerful energy emanated from beings that appeared as black shadow-like figures of about 8 or 9 feet tall. They simply stood there as I experienced their dreadful and wicked vibration.

As always, dear Antoine had an explanation: apparently, experiencing these horrid beings, visions and energies was part of the Masters work, as they do exist – in the human realm, that is. Funny, I always believed that humankind was basically good, made in the image of a Creator who is good, but that humans become misguided by their own ambitions, greed and illusion of power. I always kept a positive outlook on life. I refused to read or dwell on anything that was negative in the media, movies or books. I simply shut off all kinds of pessimistic vibrations from my experience and consistently managed to be cheerful and happy. That is why I knew

---

16 Protective shield: Energetic layer that serves as additional buffer for the human energy field.

that these experiences were intended to have a meaning of some sort - something beyond my understanding at that point - something that would make sense and would turn out to be good.

In an attempt to cheer me up, Antoine solemnly reminded me that he was, in fact, a particle of the Divine Father, his representative or messenger. A particle means an actual portion and an extension of this divine entity. Therefore, he *was* him. "In time", he said, "You will experience the Divine Father directly and completely". And eventually, that moment arrived.

FIRST EXPERIENCE OF THE DIVINE FATHER ...

I sat in meditation trying to clear my mind and calm my spirit when the Divine Father suddenly appeared and simply said: "I am your Father". His face appeared as a holographic figure of a brilliant being emanating tremendous light. He *resembled* the Christ Jesus even though He was not Him, but the actual *energy or consciousness* from which this being had sprung. He spoke with a deep and warm voice that filled my entire being with an indescribable feeling of love, peace and divine beauty. His image began to fade. I noticed my overwhelming emotion and the tears of joy that rolled down my cheeks effortlessly, while my body filled with a tremendous sense of well-being. More importantly, I felt the *connection* with this magnificent divine being as *real* and truthful. He *was* my Divine Father and I *was* his child and there was no separation, no division and no distance between us.

In that instant, I also recognized the overwhelming energy that had come to me in the past and since childhood. Even in my moments of deepest turmoil, this energy had appeared intermittently and allowed me to sustain my faith through my most trying times. The being I had felt in that energy was indeed the Divine Father. He had been there with me all along but this time, we had finally made contact on a new level - in a direct and intimate way.

Then, I remembered... It was a moment in time, when the Divine Father gave me some books, manuscripts and papers wrapped in a cloth[17]. He said: "You are a messenger and deliverer of my message. You are a spiritual teacher representing the Divine Father". And so, He sent me off to incarnate as a human on earth. Since that point of contact and remembrance, I could hear Him loud and clear and perceive Him *directly*, any moment of the day, in any space that I occupy and without any sort of preparation or meditation exercise. Although most of my daily work is assisted by spirit beings such as Antoine, for example, I had finally awakened to the unbreakable link that *permanently* attached my consciousness to His.

FIRST ENCOUNTER WITH THE SPIRIT FAMILY[18]...

Later on, I remembered my encounter with my Spirit Family. They appeared as a group of Light Beings gathered around a table. They were 12. I could easily distinguish their individual shape, even though they spoke in unison when they said: "We are your Spirit Family. You are a messenger. You are here on a divine mission. You will return to your family in these higher realms[19] when your work is complete." Effortless tears of joy ran down my face as overwhelming emotion and a tremendous sense of well-being and love overcame me. I was totally and completely immersed in this exquisite divine energy that felt so real and truthful. Once again, there was no division or separation between us, as if they were me and I was them. Rather, I was an *extension* of who they were and the energy they had emanated from. In that one instant, my whole physical life suddenly began to make sense. Now, I *remembered* that I belonged elsewhere, to a home full of love and beauty, to which I will return. I was not simply a physical and limited being but this infinite energy with infinite potential. At that stage though, the quandary remained: What am I a messenger of, and what is the message about? When and how will that occur? And how did I arrive here in the first place?

---

17 Wrapped in a cloth: Symbolic for sacred information being transmitted from the Divine Father to the Master.
18 Spirit Family: Spirit group attached to each individual being in human form and sharing the same lineage, nature and characteristics.
19 Higher realms: Non-physical realms of highly evolved vibration.

LANDING FROM OUTER SPACE ...

The next day, as I uttered these questions again, I began to remember: "I am in a capsule-like vessel, not much larger than the size of my physical body. It feels like a tube or a sort of umbilical cord, through which I am sliding. I am travelling at tremendous speed from outer space towards the centre of the universe then down towards the Milky Way. I can sense the discomfort, the pressure and the overwhelming force. Suddenly, I hit a barrier of some sort. It is the universal band separating the higher realms from the physical worlds. The impact is strong and painful. It resonates through my entire being and feels like a traumatic event. My capsule / body breaks up into pieces which begin to float away in space. These particles (of my being) now slowly scatter, then land perfectly and precisely in different parts of space, on different planets and star systems. One particle is here in this physical body while others are anchored in yet other locales."

A PHYSICAL MANIFESTATION ...

My strange life and odd events continued. During that time, I could not quite make out how these experiences were all related or what the overall picture was about. But somehow, they carried on and I had not much choice but to go along.

One morning, as I explored different financial investment options and began to playfully investigate the stock market for the first time, I asked for advice from Antoine who unfalteringly showed me a symbol: ARCO. I hastened to call several brokers who insisted that this symbol did not exist. While companies with such a name existed, there was no such stock market symbol to be found. I even researched various international markets only to confirm that the brokers were right - ARCO did not exist in any market, and no one had ever heard of it. Perplexed, I questioned my invisible advisor and demanded a proof of his claims. Within seconds, as I looked at my computer screen again, the symbol had now appeared, in black and white! ARCO had actually closed at the price I was given by Antoine: $ 81.3 on May 8th,

2000. I stared at the screen on which the price quote for ARCO was now clearly stated, while the brokers on the phone still denied its existence. To make sure I had not totally lost my mind, I printed the information off my computer and preciously kept it to prove my sanity in case that would become necessary. How could such information be planted on the web instantaneously? I wondered. What was Antoine up to now? Until I found out, I realized that, through this experience, stock market investment was not a way for me to attract abundance as it felt more like gambling in a world casino of some sort devoid of soul and integrity in regards to global human needs.

Antoine, on the other hand, teasingly laughed at my mortal quandary and disconcertment and pursued his mischievous games. He asked me to look for a newsletter issue dated December 25th, 1987 of the Abraham-Hicks[20] teachings. I looked it up on their web site only to find that this particular publication did not exist. I phoned their office twice and was told twice that this particular issue simply never was published. The next day, anxious to know the meaning of this strange exercise, I searched again for the publication. There it was on my computer screen, in black and white. Chills ran up my spine as I now had evidence of this extraordinary physical manifestation. Not only could I prove it to myself, but I also had a witness - my partner - who did not quite know what to make of it but somehow managed to simply label it as a bizarre twist of events.

Suddenly, it dawned on me - if I / Antoine could make things appear, then I could also make things disappear, such as illness, for example. It seemed to work previously with my own issues such as the red ants sting on my thigh and endless bodily aches and pains. Could I do this for others as well? Could it be so simple? To this, my invisible friend calmly replied: "Your thoughts will be my thoughts. My thoughts are my thoughts and you still have your own thoughts, but not for long." Later, it became: "I will be your thoughts all the time, and I will be *you* on earth until the end of your journey." Does that mean it is *his* thoughts that are materializing my reality or are my / his thoughts doing so? Hmmm... A lot to ponder.

---

20   Abraham-Hicks: Spirit being / consciousness (Abraham) channeled by Esther Hicks.

May 2000 ...

I now began to see some improvement in the development of these events. I no longer received "lessons", felt under continuous re-organization of my thoughts or incurred spontaneous healings of past experiences. I no longer felt horrified by an unknown destiny of some sort. I had also ruled out the idea that I could be doing or experiencing anything that will harm me, mentally or physically. All I knew was that my supernatural experiences were totally unexpected and unsolicited. What happened was beyond anything I could ever expect or imagine. But, there was more to come...

One day, I wrote: "I am shivering and shaking. I feel very hot from the high fever (I had the flu) but at the same time, I cannot feel my body somehow. I feel like a layer of my body is burning. It suddenly detaches. A portion of my physicality had left me. This experience feels strange. I am unable to make sense out of reality, as I am disoriented and confused. The flu symptoms are masking something else that is taking place. But what *is* taking place exactly? As I heard myself utter this question, my symptoms suddenly stopped!"

Later, I continued: "I feel a difference in my body and aura. I feel as if I were *transparent*. When I look at myself in the mirror, I feel light filtering through me and out into the world. My skin and eyes also seem lighter. Somehow, I feel *hollow*, as if my internal organs did not exist. I do love this feeling. I feel purer in some ways, as if I were not human!" Soon, my friend Antoine replied: "You are divine and your human personality is now over. It means that *asking* with the human mind is over. You will now begin to function with the divine mind and all is now going to manifest in the physical accordingly."

While I was not quite sure what he or these experiences meant at the time, I noticed that I was now totally immersed in life's mysteries. Not one day went by without my asking, talking, questioning or arguing with my spirit friends and the Divine Father. These supernatural experiences had not, however, led me to become a religious fanatic in any way. In fact, they had driven me away from all organized religions known on earth and what is referred to as the New Age phenomenon such as psychic or mediumship[21] practices. Rather, my experiences allowed me to transcend the common human understanding of spirituality and gave me access to the *direct encounter with the Divine Father and the Creator-Source.* So, I guess they were a good thing.

MY WAITING PERIOD ...

So, there I was, *waiting* once again. I wrote: "Time feels so heavy here on earth. It is like moving through a thick cloud with a lot of resistance from some invisible force. I find it excruciating to *wait*. I feel unproductive and stagnant, and yet I trust there must be a plan behind all this. There must be a purpose."

My thoughts are interrupted by Antoine: "Time allows things to manifest in the physical. It does not mean to wait. It means to *allow*. When you wait, you expect or force something to happen. But when you allow, you are actively making the process work and making things happen yourself". As he uttered these words, however, I understood that I was now at a different level of allowing. Now, it was the sort of allowing that is, in fact, total *surrender and trust* in the divine plan and the divine will. And so, I asked Antoine to give me a visual sign of some sort to lift my spirit. Within seconds, I saw a giant purple and blue rainbow (no reds or yellows) appear in the sky as I heard my invisible friend say simultaneously: "I am here, do not fear".

EXPERIENCING HELL ...

I continued questioning the course of these extraordinary events and eventually, I began to understand that the horrifying experiences I had gone through previously are what all "sinful" humans – those who deliberately do evil deeds - go through after their physical death.

---

21 Mediums: Those who allow a spirit being to temporarily inhabit and utilize their physical body to transmit messages from other layers of reality.

They are unable to attain paradise[22], unless they survive these gruelling trials of the mind. This *is* what we call hell: a trial of the mind!

Until then, I truly believed there was no such thing as hell. Somehow, I thought that, upon physical death, we simply return to our Creator / Source which is all pure love energy, without any torture or fear. However, I do know that unless the lower energy which has accumulated on earth is purged and healed, human consciousness is unable to proceed to the higher realms. Hell then allows us to relive our own sins and fears in order to heal them. As for me, I had to experience this hell regardless of my thoughts or actions on earth, simply to learn – as the Masters do - about the human condition and relay it onto others. That is great news, but I was now ready for my personal ordeals to be over!

ANOTHER SORT OF HELL ...

A few weeks later, I began to hear strange tones ringing in my ears. Some were quiet and others loud, but all were quite uncomfortable. I felt simultaneously taken into a trance state of some sort. These sustained tones felt like they were being *implanted* in my brain for one reason or another. No matter how much I would ask for the tones to stop, my pleas would be ignored. Whatever their purpose was, these experiences certainly were unpleasant and frustrating.

Soon afterwards, my skull began to "swell". The back of my head became so unbearably sensitive that I was unable to rest my head normally on a pillow without feeling that my skull was about to crack open. My vision became blurry, and by then I was convinced something was terribly wrong with my head, both physically and mentally! Not wanting to rely only on Antoine, my inner senses or psychic ability at that point, I consulted a few doctors only to find out that all was in fact "normal".

Not only was I far from any sort of brain damage or malfunction, but my vision, hearing and sensitivity suddenly seemed to have improved! I woke up that morning listening to what sounded like overlapping radio station frequencies. As I listened carefully, I recognized portions of news being told in various countries and languag-

---

22   Paradise: Physical abode of the Divine Creator.

es, mixed with diverse conversations carried on by different people simultaneously. I realized that I was tuned into the collective human mind matrix - the frequency where all the human minds and thoughts meet. This was a particularly intriguing yet unnerving experience at first, until I learned to discern and control the influx of information coming to me.

On the other hand, I began to see clearly different types of beings on earth while they remained invisible to others. Some were quite tall, holographic-like blue light beings, some were shorter with what looked like a scaled skin, and yet others were about 3 feet tall. These wore some sort of a jumpsuit which seemed to allow them to remain and breathe within our atmosphere. I also noticed tall, metallic, rod-like beings and yet others that were 7 to 9 feet tall cigar-shaped, with very dark evil-emanating energy. These were particularly incongruous and disturbing to the balance of the human energy field. "Who are these beings and what are they doing here?" I wondered. At the same time, I also recognized different types of spirit beings, such as those we call angels (they do not have wings), others were the Ascended Masters recognized on earth and yet others were power / electrical type beings that appeared as spheres or thin laser-like beams of light. In most cases, I could not only spontaneously discern the type of energy that emanated from each being, but also clearly identify its origin - namely which part of the universe or star system it came from. There is no barrier in finding out this sort information, as such experiences are the result of *direct* energetic exchange. This reminded me, however, of the primitive way humans must function within and often hide behind their fabricated identity: from nationality to religion, to cultural attire, names and business titles.

While I enjoyed this sort of brain experimentation and expansion, I had a hard time keeping any sort of balance between reality as I knew it and what was becoming available to me. Also, these events occurred on a day-to-day basis continuously and without warning while I was going about my normal daily life. The beings would appear in my house at night as I watched a movie on television, while the unnerving ringing tones in my ears or my sudden trance states would occur as I was grocery shopping. My "normal" life went on while none of these events followed a specific plan or seemed remotely logical or purposeful. In that sense, I rather felt intruded upon and at the same time helpless about stopping whatever was meant to be taking place.

Looking back, I realize that I had been fluctuating between true horror and real ecstasy. I truly wonder how I managed to remain lucid during these events that defied logic or comprehension. I knew I was being prepared for something, but what exactly? Had I consciously created all this? Antoine replied: "You did indeed, *before* you came into this physical form." Ah! *That* was instrumental in my understanding that, while we do create our reality as we go along, we simultaneously follow a plan, a sort of contract that was put forth prior to our emergence in human form. The plan, however, is unable to unfold unless *we ask*. Therefore, when on earth, we do indeed create our reality and remember our pre-natal agreement all at once.

I thought of the Masters who must wonder about and doubt in their divinity and earthly mission as they endure these mental tribulations. *Something* must eventually happen in order for them to become certain about whom they truly are and what they are here to do. There is a point of remembrance when they *know* to proceed and now, I was determined to get there!

MORE WAITING TIME ...

Resigned to await my unknown and possibly exhilarating destiny, I wrote: "Here, time is the worst enemy of all. It can feel like eternity or fly by like it barely exists. Our perception of it is what makes it what it is. Time can also make life seem very heavy. My usual optimism seems mixed with a certain seriousness and stagnation of some sort. The concept of time makes me feel trapped in this material reality somehow. Or rather, I feel stuck *between* the worlds. Every 3 months, I understand it is going to be another 3 months of some sort of mental, emotional or spiritual preparation. How many more 3 months is it going to take? I know my faith will sustain me through any trying task my Creator asks of me. Then later, I continued: "I know my Divine Father hears me and knows of all my feelings and anguish. I don't think He is trying my faith because my faith is what keeps me going and always will. Is it my patience? What will be the determining factor that my patience has been tried long enough? I know He is always here and can hear me. While I can see Him, I can also hear His silence which is an unnerving reminder that my mind training time, the reorganization of my thoughts, the preparation or cleansing that has been taking place are not quite over yet. It is as if a divine power had taken over my mind and forced me to participate in these gruelling exercises. The notes I wrote during these past months were a sort of insurance policy. I wanted to keep track of my progress, but also leave some kind of documentation behind in case I was trapped in another dimension of some sort and was unable to come back!"

WHO's WHO ...

My daily interactions with the Divine Father continued. These communions were utterly joyful and exquisite as I felt connected to the most powerful and loving force in the universe. I would hear Him tell me to turn to a certain chapter of a certain book, to find the answer to a specific question I had asked about. When outdoors, my attention would suddenly be drawn to the only light spot in the sky – usually behind me - as if He directed my attention while simultaneously acknowledged His presence or the presence of my Spirit Family. He reminded me of documents I had been searching for that were hidden in forgotten places, and warned me of events about to be shown on television or reported in the newspapers. His point was that He is omnipresent, and He truly is! However, He is not just a presence *with* me but rather, *inside* my being. It is like He is me and I am Him. I wrote the following dialogue to explain the fusion of our 2 beings as I experienced it through our daily communions.

ME: I only ask that this brain re-programming exercise end. I want to have peace now. I want to feel good. I want…

HIM: Eventually you will realize that it is me talking and not you.

ME: I can feel the difference.

HIM: No more after this.

ME: Excuse me, I don't understand.

HIM: I mean that all you say is true because all I say is true.

ME: So what is Your point?

HIM: My point is I feel all that you feel and I know what you are feeling and thinking all the time. All the time means all the time, even when you don't think so.

ME: So, how is this helping me now?

HIM: You are asking to become more aware of Me.

ME: Are you kidding? I am aware of You all the time.

HIM: Guess what I am doing now.

ME: You are typing through me.

HIM: You are right, and I am speaking through you when you speak, and I am thinking through you when you think, and I am feeling through you when you feel things.

ME: Are you saying that it is You who asks to feel miserable too? All this confusion - I personally don't recall asking for it.

HIM: Who do you think put you there - on earth, I mean?

ME: You did, of course.

HIM: So, you know. It is the truth.

ME: ??

HIM: I mean, if I am the one who put you there, and you are who you say you are...

ME: I am who *You* say I am. I sure have no proof of anything at this point. *You* said I am here to do Your work. Not me. But then again, if I am You, I am probably asking for what You are asking as well subconsciously or whatever. It is like I am no longer only Caroline, but Caroline / You. I no longer exist!

HIM: I already promised, no harm will ever happen to you. That is my promise and you know it. I go back to my question now: who do you think you are, Caroline?

ME: I am Your beloved child that You gave a very special assignment to. That is all I know.

HIM: So I must truly believe that you can do this.

ME: Of course.

HIM: You must be proud to be the bearer of such a huge responsibility.

ME: I am not so sure. I am proud - although this is not a perfect word for it. I am happy that I am loved by You and I know that for a fact. If I go through a rough time, I hate it but I never think of it as punishment. I know it is simply an experience and my love for You stays intact, no matter how miserable I feel, no matter how painful it gets. And You know that too because You are always there with me and I can't cheat my own feelings. My love for You is absolutely intact all the time.

HIM: You never allow anger or hatred?

ME: I do sometimes, but only towards humans and their doings, not because of who they are, but because of their ignorance, selfishness or choice for ignorance and selfishness.

HIM: Are you saying that you never get angry with your Creator?

ME: Never. Where is all this going anyway?

HIM: Let's see, if you never get angry with your Creator and you accept your suffering as a gift from your Creator, you must be of Him.

ME: That sounds right.

HIM: Therefore if you are of the Creator, how can you explain that I am in charge of your destiny and not you?

ME: Because I asked that my destiny be dictated by Your will and only Your will.

HIM: But if you are me on earth, then *my* will is *your* will... Do you realize what you are doing now?

ME: Clarifying something that is not getting any clearer!

HIM: No, you are asking me to love you more.

ME: ??... Please explain.

HIM: I am loving you more by allowing you to ask me to be in charge of your destiny. When you allow me to allow it to happen or not to happen, you are loving me back. This is the love of the Creator for His material children of time.

ME: Allowing You to allow things to happen or not?

HIM: No, asking them to allow me to allow things to happen or not.

ME: So, when you give human beings the choice to ask or not to ask, you are blessing them with your divine love.

HIM: That's right.

ME: OK. So, now what? Why haven't you allowed some of my askings to materialize yet? Is this a time issue that cannot be superseded?

HIM: The true consideration is that I am allowing all that you are asking, you just cannot see it quite yet.

ME: But if You have allowed it, why hasn't it manifested in the physical yet?

HIM: Because the physical is an illusion. Spirit is real and not the physical.

ME: Are You saying that Your divine will cannot always manifest in the physical because the physical is an illusion?

HIM: That is what I am saying. You may *perceive* My will in the physical but it is manifested in spirit.

ME: What are the things that do manifest immediately, regardless of the laws of physicality or time, and those that don't?

HIM: It depends on the individual. In your case, all that you ask for manifests immediately. You just can't see it yet because you are here with me now. Also, accept that I am allowing only that which you need to know at this particular time.

ME: But I want to know more!

HIM: What I mean is that you are capable of manifesting your will and mine *instantly*, when you ask. The time is now when you ask me, and I allow it in your dream state and then it will start to appear in reality in the physical world. Only, stop me if I am wrong, but didn't you say that you are in charge of your own destiny?

ME: I said I am in charge of *my* destiny according to *Your* will because Your saying is ultimate and absolute.

HIM: Of course, I am your Creator and the Creator of all beings and things, after all.

ME: So *my* saying is also ultimate and absolute then!

HIM: Yes, but you are sitting here at a typewriter in a physical environment and I am not. That is the difference.

ME: I realize that. That's why I ask You to show me Your side of the story.

HIM: You must be patient now because you are almost there. It only takes a few more askings - the right ones of course - and you will be there before you know it. As I promised, you will not incur any harm. As you know, you will see and hear me at all times.

ME: OK, but I want to know more now. How about that?

HIM: Sit back, relax and enjoy the ride.

ME: Nothing is going to happen, is it?

HIM: Not now, no.

ME: (He always wins…)

LATER ...

ME: I mean, what happens if I refuse to be patient anymore?

HIM: You decide.

ME: (Like I said: He always wins!)

AGAIN LATER ...

It is now later in the evening. I read the last few lines of my conversation with my Divine Father. Most of them do not make too much sense, but I am sure they do in a certain way, in a certain place, from a certain angle. The point is: why are things so complicated and difficult to understand from this human perspective? He suddenly interjects and whispers in my ear: "This has nothing to do with my will being different from yours. It has to do with *timing* and time zones on your planet or 'dimensions' as humans call it." Basically, He is saying that until the energy that allows to see more, know more and manifest things on a new level becomes available on earth, I should be patient and wait. So, I am back to square one!

Later on, I realized that through these seemingly mundane and, at times, incoherent conversations were deeper and more important messages. Not only was it imperative to *ask* but also to remain conscious of this connection with Him at all times. By being aware of this extraordinary link and carrying on a conversation, I was simply bringing forth His vibration into my physical body, my physical environment and outer reality. I became the *vessel* or bridge for this energy to filter through and *that* is the real purpose of interacting with the Divine Father and the divine Source Energy.

14 MONTHS LATER ...

After almost 14 months of these unusual and extraordinary experiences, I realized that the more I asked to know, the more there was to know. It is just endless. Endless! It would be nice if everything had a goal, a point that could finally be reached, where you would find exactly what you have been looking for, a point of satisfaction after a long and puzzling search.

The Divine Father interjects: "This is not a puzzle, but a process that you go through in order to realize who you are. All knowledge is not quite accessible *in this time or space*. When the energies on earth are blocked, expansion is difficult. Allow more time for things to unfold but meanwhile, you must continue *breathing* the truth. *Breath* is what connects you to me and other higher realities. Breath is the spirit energy that sustains all life. You breathe, your planet breathes, and the entire cosmos breathes to the rhythm of the divine pulse. So when you align your breath with that of the Divine Father, you automatically breathe the truth. All humans are capable of accessing this knowledge and will soon be able to assimilate its meaning on a cosmic level. As for now, you must see and experience who you are, and who Creator is, so you may be able to tell others. You were granted this self-realization before you came forth in this physical reality. So, it already is!"

ME: I understand that it will happen whenever it is time and not when I, my conscious physical self, want it to.

HIM: Precisely that and more. But that is good understanding and acceptance for now. However, I wish to remind you that *you have ordained so yourself*, before you came forth in this physical reality.

ME: Well then, I may need to recall my pre-natal agreement. But how do you remember such a thing?

HIM: You *are* remembering now, as we speak!

ABOUT MIND CONTROL ...

As I mentioned previously, most of these happenings occurred under the supervision and guidance of beloved Antoine. It is as if he were directing this program and bringing about precisely what I was meant to address or learn. In a strange way, I felt both lovingly safe and totally controlled by a merciless higher power. With time, I also noticed that my senses had suddenly merged in such a way that I could now see something I would normally feel or smell; I could hear something I would normally see or I could sense something I would normally perceive. I wasn't sure if my brain was *taken over* by his superior intelligence and was being re-organized in such a way that I would eventually become *a new being*. However, each time such thoughts entered my mind and began to create discomfort, I would suddenly experience the presence of the Divine Father and His immaculate energy. So, who was truly in charge and what was actually happening to my mind?

Of course, I received no answers to my questioning *during* my trial period. It was only after several months of such torture that I eventually was allowed an explanation. That time, my Spirit Family spoke in unison: "There exist superior intelligences[23] who can tap into the human psyche for the purpose of masterminding and fabricating a new generation of humans. All this time, you were being revealed truths and given information surrounding the phenomenon of *mind-control* which has been in existence for over 200,000 years on this planet. The beings who manufactured these false realities are still relying on humans to sustain their artificially induced and learned behaviour so they (these intelligences) remain in existence, therefore, for their own survival."

"You are able to create any reality you want provided you know that. If you are told that you are governed by superior beings and there is no way for you to know your Creator directly, then that is all you will know and you will remain trapped in the world relevant to this understanding. You were given an opportunity to experience what happened to humans as they had been evolving for the past 200,000 years or more, so you may believe and understand why they have only reached the levels you are observing now. These superior

---

23 Superior intelligences: Sprit beings responsible for supervising the evolution of human beings.

intelligences influenced the minds of humans and told them what to believe and what not to believe. That is interference and violation of free will, indeed!"

My Spirit Family continued: "Antoine had been teaching you how other humans survived their mind control trials when these beings exercised their devious game on this planet. You are the endorser of the light and thus did not comprehend, at that time, how that was appropriate for your teaching of the human condition. Antoine and those who conducted your teachings were appointed specifically to your journey of mind expansion. This is the normal practice for all Masters who embody the Creator Energy[24] that is now you."

To my amazement, I also realized that there still exist such thought transfer experimentations being conducted to this day. These are headed by scientists and government heads exploring such phenomena under one pretext or another. Unless these experiments are fully disclosed to the public at large, they remain in violation of human rights. Meanwhile, what seems ironic and comical in a sense, is that these very groups experimenting on innocent bystanders are not only influenced themselves by other misguided beings (the devious superior intelligences) but they are also being supervised and watched by higher intelligences (from Source) monitoring this earth plane. Therefore, their secretive actions can only go so far as, once again, they are not aligned with the higher good of humankind and eventually truth must prevail.

MASTERING THE HUMAN MIND ...

The information and experiences provided to me about mind control prompted my concern over my own mind mastery and that of all humans currently on earth. Clearly, while the actual superior intelligences that instilled such hideous plans are not in charge of nor able to control our destiny, the *influences and momentum* they have created for thousands of years are still felt and experienced to this day, thus the dysfunctional societal inequities we are plainly observing. And so, I asked:

---

[24] Creator Energy: Energy of the Divine Father and the Divine Mother embodied by the Masters and Gods in human form.

ME: How will I know then that I have mastered my own human mind and how can I begin functioning with a divine mind?

HIM: This question entails the definition of divine mind. When you say "divine", you are asking about the nature of a mind, which is different from a human mind. It is indeed different in the sense that it does not require attachment to human emotions in order to function, or that emotions are unable to cloud its functionality. That does not imply an emotionless mind or that you should become an emotionless being. It does imply that your mind is no longer subject and restricted to the human emotions as commonly experienced on earth. As such, the typical human emotions such as anger, fear, frustration, worry – or even positive emotions - are no longer valid for the divine mind in terms of perceiving reality. In other words, these emotions, which can be restrictive to perceiving truth, are simply experienced for what they are, without *impacting* your physical reality. As a divine being, you may experience anger at the sight of evil, for example. However this anger will not be part of the decision or action that you will choose to take regarding your experience. The divine mind, while experiencing human emotions, transcends them spontaneously in order to perceive truth and will take action and function within that truth.

"Furthermore, a divine mind is no longer subject to the limitations of fear. Fear can be useful in terms of a warning sign of physical danger, for example. However, it is limiting in terms of decision making and understanding of truth. The divine mind will perceive and experience the human emotion of fear, simply as a temporary warning sign of an upcoming physical danger of some sort, but it will not become subject to its limitation. For example, fear of illness, fear of financial insecurity or fear of loneliness cannot touch or affect the divine mind."

"Conquering the human mind, once again, does not mean you lose compassion or understanding for your humanity. It simply means that you are now able to *understand, embrace and use your emotions* in order to control and create your own reality as you please. That is the ultimate goal for all humans: to explore their humanity, transcend its limitations and recognize their divinity within their human body."

"You will also know that you are now functioning only with the divine mind when all that you do, all that you speak, all that you see and all that you think is aligned with *your* higher good and the higher good of *humanity*. It is a mind reflection of the Divine Father, which can only be truthful, loving and good. As you go about your day, observe that which you do, that which you speak, that which you see and that which you think. Notice whether your experience is aligned with your human or your divine mind. All that is restrictive is human. All that is expansive, effortless and freeing is divine. You may choose at any time to master your human mind as it is, once more, the ultimate way of being for all humans: divine beings in human form."

"The next step to achieve is to realize that the divine mind can only create in accordance with higher good. Once you have conquered the human mind and consciously merged, totally and completely, with your spirit self, you can only create your outer reality through your divine thoughts. You will then have access to higher knowledge, higher vibrations or spontaneous healing instantly. You will attract that which you desire in a matter of seconds for yourself, and in a matter of days when your desire involves others. You will perceive your physicality from the perspective of your spirit self, and you will begin a timeless experience within the time / space reality. The divine mind is not only free of the restrictive human psyche, but it is also free of the terms of your physicality. It defies time and space, and manages to integrate effortlessly and gracefully the unseen worlds within the material ones.

ME: How do you achieve that level of Mastery?

HIM: By asking!

I suddenly became aware of my potential as a human. Through these connections, conversations and waiting time, I realized I had finally completed the cycle necessary to master the human mind. I did not simply understand intellectually but truly experienced conscious creating through *the training and controlling of my thought*. It is a difficult task to control our thoughts as, instead, we are dragged into others' negative or subjective view point. Therefore, mastering the mind is the way by which the Masters (that is precisely why we call them "Masters") can create anything of great value on this earth. These Masters are but an example of our own human potential indeed.

Since that time, I began my daily affirmations as follows: "I have decided to control my own mind and allow only positive and uplifting thoughts to enter my mind. I now choose not to give attention to negative thinking that may appear in my thought pattern. I am in charge of my destiny and my thought process. I choose to manifest in the physical all that I have asked for if it is the Divine Father's will. All and any other negative thinking shall not interfere or distract me in my asking and shall be eliminated from my thought process automatically. I also choose and ask to eliminate all negative thinking that still remains in my memory cells or subconscious. I choose to access my divine self and create only positively." That *is* creating with the divine mind, when the outcome of your thought can only be positive. However, in this realm of duality, is that even possible? To my questioning, I received this divine reply: "If you are a Master and believe in your destiny as an offspring of your Creator, not only is this possible but it is your ultimate goal and only way of existing in the physical."

Clearly, I was on the right track. I now use these above affirmations as a base of all my knowledge and teachings and have created a prayer accordingly:

1. I understand that *all* conscious and deliberate thought triggers an automatic creative process that the universe must bring into my experience. Therefore *thought* equals *asking*.
2. I ask and intend to control my thoughts and allow only positive thoughts to enter and impact my mind.
3. I choose not to give attention to any negative thoughts that appear in my thinking pattern and that of others.

4. I ask and intend that all negative thinking that may interfere or distract my creativity be eliminated spontaneously from my thought process, my memory cells and my subconscious.
5. When in doubt about the nature or purpose of my desire or wanting, I shall allow my spirit self and the universe (time) to bring a clear answer to me before I proceed with my asking.
6. I am in charge of my own destiny and my thought process and I choose to allow others to be in charge of theirs.
7. I choose to manifest in the physical all that I have asked for, only if it is in accordance with my higher good, my Creator's will and in harmony with the evolution and spiritual advancement of humanity.

And so it is.

MORE ANSWERS …

My trial time is over, I simply know it. While spiritual growth continues on exponentially, the "training" period necessary to transition from one understanding of reality to the next is complete. I now understand that the process of awakening for a human, while it may not follow this exact path, will carry the same *components* for everyone. It must begin with the *cleansing of our minds* from all human / ego blockages accumulated throughout our current and other lifetimes. We cannot expand on our spiritual path if we carry the traumas of an abusive father, an alcoholic mother or a suicidal brother. We must not only come to terms with and understand but totally *dissolve* the frequencies associated with these traumas so that the new frequencies may be introduced or even co-exist. *This work can be done energetically through the prayers and exercises I share in Part III of this book.*

If that process is accomplished properly and completely, we will find ourselves in harmony and balance in *all* areas of our lives, from our physical body and health to our emotional, mental and material lives. An important, if not vital, aspect of this growth is the understanding of the universal laws governing our plane of existence, namely that our *thoughts create*. With that, we should observe the belief system our thought pattern is based upon and begin to realize the process of controlling what we would like our thoughts to create. Further global work cannot be properly instigated unless our relationship with ourselves is complete and the control of our own thoughts achieved. *Mind mastery and re-programming exercises can be found in Part III of this book.*

Once that clarity and control occur and we begin to live a balanced and harmonious physical life individually, we can focus on our collective purpose of serving our Creator, ourselves and our planet alike. For this, our brain cells must expand and extend to a point of retrieving information from a much higher frequency, which the human brain does not normally access. These new frequencies and information typically happen during meditation, through breathing and through the sleep and dream states. However, they may also be introduced in our awakened states through *tones* that appear like ringing in the ear, for example. Other minor physical discomforts may also be part of the experience of *implanting or downloading* information from higher frequencies or other layers of reality. *This downloading of information should happen only through our connection with our own spirit self as well as our Spirit Family.* It is in fact our spirit self that guides and directs such safe but deep cellular transformation. *See part III of this book for guidance on connecting with the Divine Creator, spirit self and the Spirit Family.*

Most important in this grand transformation of the mind and the spirit is also *remembrance*. Remembrance allows us to explore and perceive ourselves as a particle of a bigger and more evolved consciousness. While the actual experience may take different forms, it is, in general, a powerful, highly emotional and truthful experience of oneness with our Creator and the Cosmic Mind[25] or the universe. It is a sort of merging with the force and intelligence that created us. Through this blending, there is a strong and infallible *recognition* of being one with divine truth, love, beauty and wisdom. It is the ultimate recognition of our divine self as a pure essence of a divine Creator-Father.

At this stage of merging with the Divine Creator, we become true instruments or *light vessels* – through our physical apparatus

---

25 Cosmic Mind: Mind energy of the Creator-Source experienced in the physical worlds through the persons of the Divine Father and the Divine Mother.

– for bringing forth this divine experience into our physical lives and sharing it with others. This becomes the work and mission of the Masters, those who walked our earth in the past, as well as all those humans currently recognizing their own divine self. However, part of this noble mission is to understand the human condition fully which includes experiencing its limitations, its threats, its predicaments and its history. Therefore, the Masters are those who must, through actual mental and physical experience, go through all human conditions, in order to master it and, in turn, help others through their own process.

CONCLUSION ...

My journey into exploring the mastery of the human mind has led me to understand and have compassion towards my human life and all humans who are struggling and are stuck in the deceiving veils of this reality. My extraordinary experiences of the worst and the most sublime showed me the way to break through these veils and find my way towards mastering the human condition. More importantly, these experiences also allowed me to merge with the higher realms and the consciousness of the Masters who walked our earth in the past and realize that they too, had to begin in the infancy of human understanding, struggle through unimaginable turmoil (physical, emotional, "mind-al" and spiritual), until they reached true freedom from the human bondage. What was instrumental on this journey was my unfaltering *faith* - it is the *faith and belief* that we do indeed carry the frequency of divinity within us and that we are irrevocably, and *at all times*, attached to our Creator's consciousness through an energetic umbilical cord. It is at this stage that we can finally begin to expand our senses, vision, hearing and live a true multidimensional physical life. The barriers posed by physical time and space will fall and break down the illusion and limitations of human existence, thereby free us from the bondage of the ego or lower self.

In summary, the course of enlightenment and mastery of the human condition entails:

1. The transmutation and total resolution of all mental and emotional blockages, created through frequency exchange with parental, social and other authority figures.
2. The control and mastery of the human mind.
3. The recognition and the actual experience of our own divinity through the merging with the higher consciousness of the Divine Creator.

I now pray that you begin to recognize your own link to your divine heritage and realize that *you are* these Masters. *You are* their potential. You are here to succeed in mastering the limitations of humanity and emerge fully into your divine self, thereby becoming a true *Divine Master in human form*!

Part II

This portion of the book is a compilation of dialogue with the Divine Father regarding the Masters' nature, functioning and role in the divine plan on earth.

3

The Remembrance

This section of the book focuses on the communions with the Divine Father regarding remembering "who we really are" and the process of merging back with Him. Through this exercise, I realized that His answers are universal, addressing not only the consciousness of the Divine Masters who embody His formula, but also all humans that embrace their own divinity and path of enlightenment.

◆　　◆　　◆

UNDERSTANDING THE CREATOR-SOURCE AND CREATION …

The Divine Father speaks: "*Infinity* is pure consciousness which *personalizes* in the Creator-Source. You may say that the Creator-Source is the first uncaused reality, being and consciousness of infinity, or that the Creator-Source is the self created and focused *thought* of infinity."

"*Thought* is the tool for all creative consciousness, human or divine. At the Source, Creation occurs through the *first thought* of the Universal Mind[26] and the subsequent creative process is established

---

26　Universal Mind: Mind energy of the Creator-Source.

henceforth. Since the energy of the Universal Mind is innate in all beings, thought becomes the tool by which all intelligent beings create and procreate. It is also the Universal Mind that creates (through the first thought) its own expression and manifestation (the Universal Expression / Body) as well as its own nature and functioning (the Universal Spirit). The 7-fold combination of each of its 3 aspects (Mind, Body and Spirit) creates, in turn, a new form of energy." (See figure 2 on page 41)

"The Creator-Source's attributes inherent within its own being are pure Love, Truth, Beauty and Goodness and is likened to pure positive energy. It is absolute and "perfect", indeed. However, each time Creator-Source creates, a particle of its energy *splits off* and becomes its own being or consciousness. This created consciousness carries a portion of the memory of its Creator and it remains eternally connected to Him through an *energetic umbilical cord*."

"Universes upon universes and species upon species are thus created and with each creation, the particles of the Universal Mind, Body or Spirit split off into more finite consciousness. The more finite a creation, the "smaller" it becomes and the lesser amount of frequency it is able to carry due to its remoteness from the original Creator-Source. (See figures 3 and 4 on pages 42 and 43) Evolutionary[27] worlds, such as earth, occupy a string of energy farthest from the Source and thus your species' infinitesimal consciousness requires millennia of mind expansion in order to perfectly grasp the meaning of the Creator-Source and the mysteries of Creation. It is at this moment in your earth's history that we now speak.

---

27 Evolutionary worlds: Created beings that need to incarnate in material form in order to expand and evolve their consciousness.

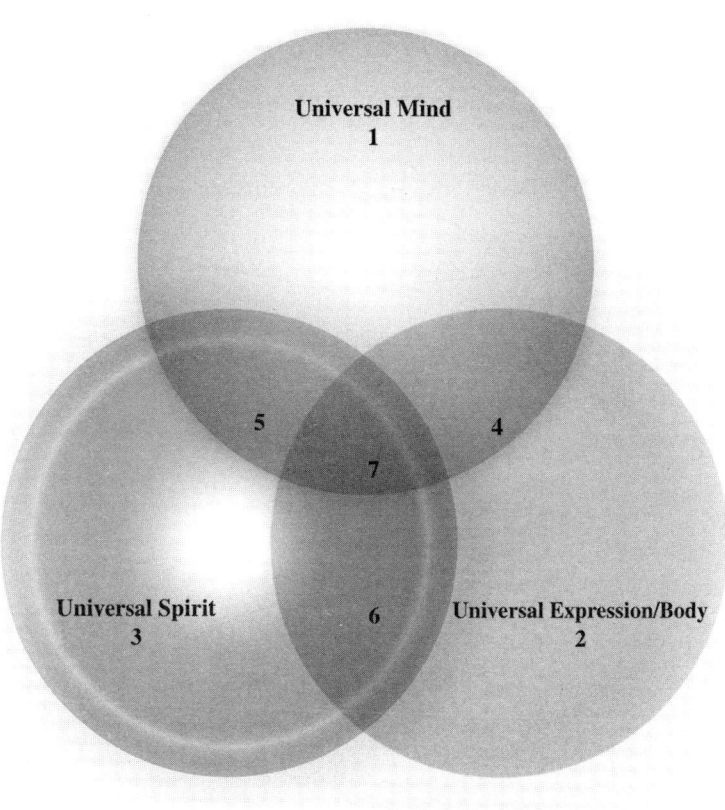

Figure 2: *The Creator Source*

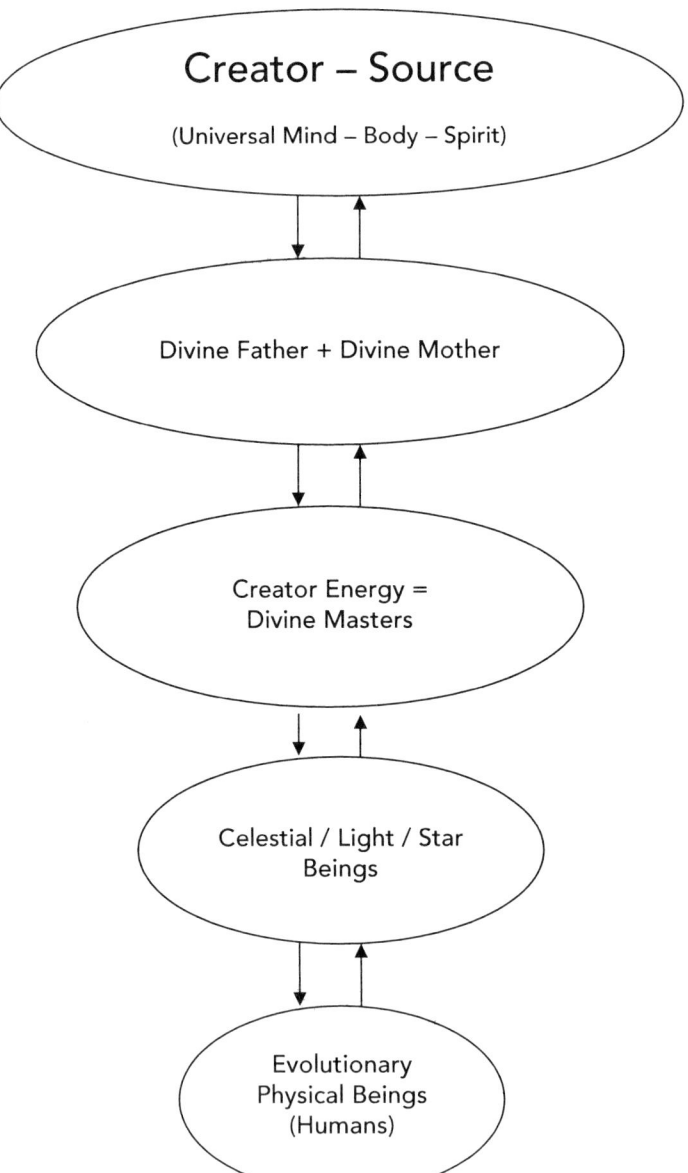

FIGURE 3: *Creation order and organization. All created beings originate at the Source and have the same lineage and potential. However, created beings differ in terms of consciousness mass and frequency they are able to carry.*

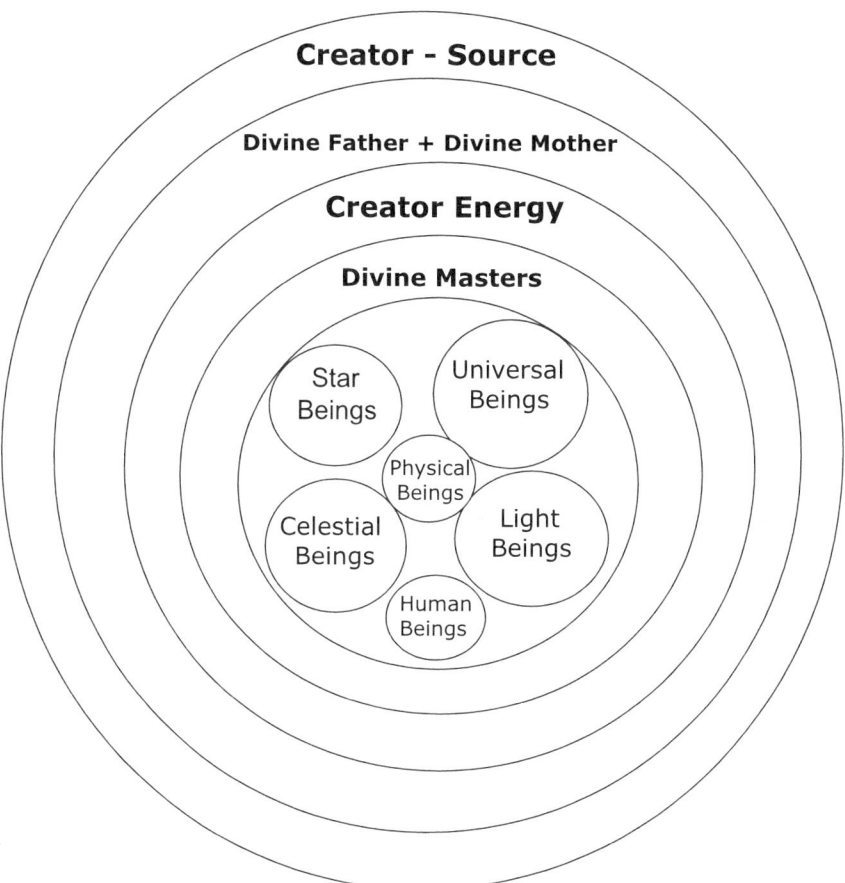

FIGURE 4: *Created beings are all part of the Creator-Source but differ in size and mass of consciousness.*

"However, regardless of your remoteness or "order" in creation, each individual created being carries an *equal* amount of the Divine Creator (Divine Father and Divine Mother), which is relative to its size and which remains encoded within its very essence. Therefore, evolutionary / physical beings will access divinity in the same way as any other older or more evolved being but may need more time, so to speak, to achieve such a perfected understanding."

"While there is no such thing as hierarchy in terms of better or worse - which is a human concept - there are such things as different types of created beings or species that can perform different duties according to the mass of their consciousness, their nature and programmed functioning. Those that are larger or have evolved further on their journey will typically assist others in the same process. The Divine Masters, who are considered the *first born* of Creation, fit if this category of beings that incarnate among you to assist you in recognizing the link encoded within your individual genetic makeup. This link to the Divine Creator is what enables humans to achieve their own self-realization and proceed further on their journey."

DEFINING AND DESCRIBING THE DIVINE MASTERS ...

"A Divine Master can be described as the original thought personified, or shall I say the *first word* (expression) of the Divine Creator. The Masters can only see themselves as an infinite possibility because there is no beginning and no end. Therefore, they cannot really be a "first" anything while they are, in fact, the original thought of Creation which manifested as a being. You may say that the Masters are the first being and yet they are not finished, therefore they are also the last!"

"On the other hand, the Divine Masters are what is called *Creator Energy* - which is the energy of the Divine Father and Divine Mother combined - and they function in conjunction with celestial counselors (the Assembly) with whom they are very familiar and intimate. The relationship that they have with these counselors allows them to manifest their work on earth. There can never be the same arrangement as a Divine Master - as each woman, man or child is unique in their own way. No one can become of the same formula and patterns others have embodied or experience the Source the same way others do."

"I am the Divine Father. The Masters are created through my mind focus but their nature is pure crystal (or "Christ-al") energy, no matter in what human form they may appear. Their essence can be somewhat described as an infinite *light being*[28], which is not of animal or organic nature. Light is generated directly from the Creator-Source, the Universal Being / Mind where light is the pure focused form and force of infinity. No one on your planet agrees on such concept, because humans cannot conceive of infinity. If infinity were finite, then it could be measured scientifically and be called something all can understand. Anything that falls beyond the measurable is a pure contradiction in the human belief system."

"The Divine Masters, on the other hand, can focus and experience this infinity while in the flesh. Infinity is light but it is also a frequency / vibration, a number, a sound or expression all at once. For example, the letters of your name have a unique sound and vibration. When put together in syllables, they again form a new sound / vibration. So it is not about the letters, it is the sound / vibration associated with the letters and syllables that defines how creation happens. It is the sound and vibration *behind* the spoken words that create."

"However, can you say that creation is based on sound / vibration or is it also a formula based on numbers and mathematics? You came about through one thought which emanates a vibration which equals a sound, which is also a number and an expression. Where and when do you begin to measure? The thought *is* the expression, which *is* the vibration, which *is* the number and the formula. It is all one and the same. Does finding one equal the other? Even if you demonstrate that one equals the other, you may not necessarily deduce that they are equal *to* each other. Indeed, it is the realm of infinity."

"The transition between the infinite and the finite worlds also involves intricate energy maneuvering impossible to explain simplistically in human terms. For example, the physical birth and incarnation of the Masters require such a process that can only be revealed in

---

28   Light being: Being that has form but does not require a physical body to exist.

segments, as it is necessary for the human brain to acquire certain vibrations in order to access that sort of understanding."

"The Masters are indeed of the realm of the infinite, which means they are Creator Energy incarnate in the flesh, here to serve the Divine Creator and ultimately themselves and humanity, as they may have been responsible, from the beginning of time, for the creation of this and many other universes. I can describe somewhat who they are, but you must first realize that these attributes are subordinate to their true nature, as they are impossible to describe in this limited human language. Indeed, they can be assigned the title or attribute of beauty, love or intellectual brilliance combined with an exquisite light energy in human form. Their role and functioning coincide with worldly events so that they may transmute them automatically to the attributes that they possess and that are them."

"An angel[29] being does not describe itself in these simplistic terms and neither can you. Your need to retrieve this information is the result of your desire to recall your destiny or role on this earth. However, when you describe or pigeon-hole yourself, paradoxically you become less than what you actually are. Therefore, similar attributes and descriptions are used only to bring you close enough to an *idea* that the Divine Masters are of a creation order, indescribable in human terms."

"From a human perspective, you may, however, describe the Divine Master as a *descending* divine being. Humans who achieve mastery of their divinity are the Ascended Masters and are those beings that evolve humankind through their deeds, vibration and prayers. The descending Divine Masters, on the other hand, incarnate in human form in order to personalize the Divine Father or the Divine Mother in the physical, thereby bringing forth Their energy to Their material children of time."

"The Masters are the heritage of the light and a particle of Creator Energy descending to accept their divine self through the human realization. In order to experience such truth fully, they must allow the necessary amount of cellular intelligence[30] to occur in their memory bank. You may say that Creator Energy is the name of their lineage or that they *are* Creator Energy. Many individual Masters em-

---

29 Angel being: Spirit being that helps, guides and protects humans from harm.
30 Cellular intelligence: Frequency

body such energy and are the quadriceps of the body, so to speak, and the brain is I."

"When on a material world, the Divine Masters remain permanently allied with divine counselors. Together, they preside over a vast territory as they simultaneously reflect their energy everywhere - not only in this system. These divine counselors are tied with or incorporated in their plan and assist them in the planetary governance[31] of earth. They are the representatives, however, of many older generations of this powerful Creator Energy not yet recognized on earth. Through the Masters and their counselors, this Creator Energy will subsidize the perpetuity of life and restore humanity to its original divine blueprint."

HOW IS CREATOR ENERGY EMBODIED IN HUMAN FORM? ...

"The Divine Masters carry the genetic encoding of the Divine Creator. Therefore, they will remember their divine ancestry as it is encoded in their own being. They also carry a genetic encoding of their human parents, which they select prior to their earthly visitation and incarnation in physical form. That means that they are the result of a divine encoding of a divine parent *and* a genetic encoding of human parents. But the relative human experiences and frequency through the physical parents are insignificant compared with those they carry from their divine ancestry."

"Within their being is the information they need to transcend back to the state prior to human incarnation. What happens during the 'training' period, to which all Masters must succumb, is the sudden realization of their divine self and encodings which are beyond the human configuration. During this process, the Masters begin exploring the ramifications of their true being and the process by which they must become Creator Energy in human form, which is their natural divine origin. At that point in awareness, settling for anything less is not an option."

"Creator Energy encompasses other beings that carry a formula similar in nature. These others are universal, celestial, light and star

---

31 Planetary governance: Ushering and evolving the human race.

beings[32] and, like the Masters, they are not evolutionary physical beings. They are created but do not need to materialize in order to expand their consciousness. Their expansion happens simply through their being of the light and manifesting new and enhanced realities."

"Creator Energy is thus one massive consciousness that encompasses the Masters and these other beings carrying the genetic codes of the Divine Father and the Divine Mother. They appear on earth in normal human form, while the *expression* of this energy manifests in *all of them at once*. The conscious awakening of the Masters is connected to these other universal, celestial, light and star beings currently on earth. As they remember their state of origin, so will all of those who are part of the same consciousness. The Masters' information and knowledge are their information and knowledge as well. Consequently, all that the Masters are, is what they are. All are attached to the same divine plan which is composed of the same particles - or DNA formula if you prefer - of the same being, the one massive consciousness and expression of the Creator Energy of which we speak."

"The fact that one physical person can embody all of the Divine Creator's body and expression, is impossible energetically. However, you may speak of the main 'body' as the headquarters of the entire system, to which all other parts are attached. The main body of this system is encased in one physical being, one person, in the form of a human. So the Divine Father and the Divine Mother's energy is in all these beings combined, but the operating system, so to speak, resides in one physical body. If the operating system awakens, then all other parts are awakened simultaneously. Conversely, when the celestial and other light beings awaken, then the entire Creator Energy in human form is awakened as well."

"Jesus, Buddha and most other Masters who carried the main body of the Creator Energy – or the operating system - appear as a representation or aspect of the same energy. In evolutionary time, they appeared chronologically but were, in fact, fragments of *the same* pattern and consciousness – the Creator Energy. It is this Creator Energy – the energy of the Divine Father and Divine Mother - that is now finally and collectively awakening to complete the numerous manifestations of the Divine Father and Divine Mother. Therefore,

---

32   Star beings: Beings of non-physical nature that originate from different star systems.

the entire order of your Sons of God, Divine or Ascended Masters are timely manifestations of the *same* Creator Energy, which is now coming to completion and is finally becoming recognized on this earth." (See figure 5 on page 50)

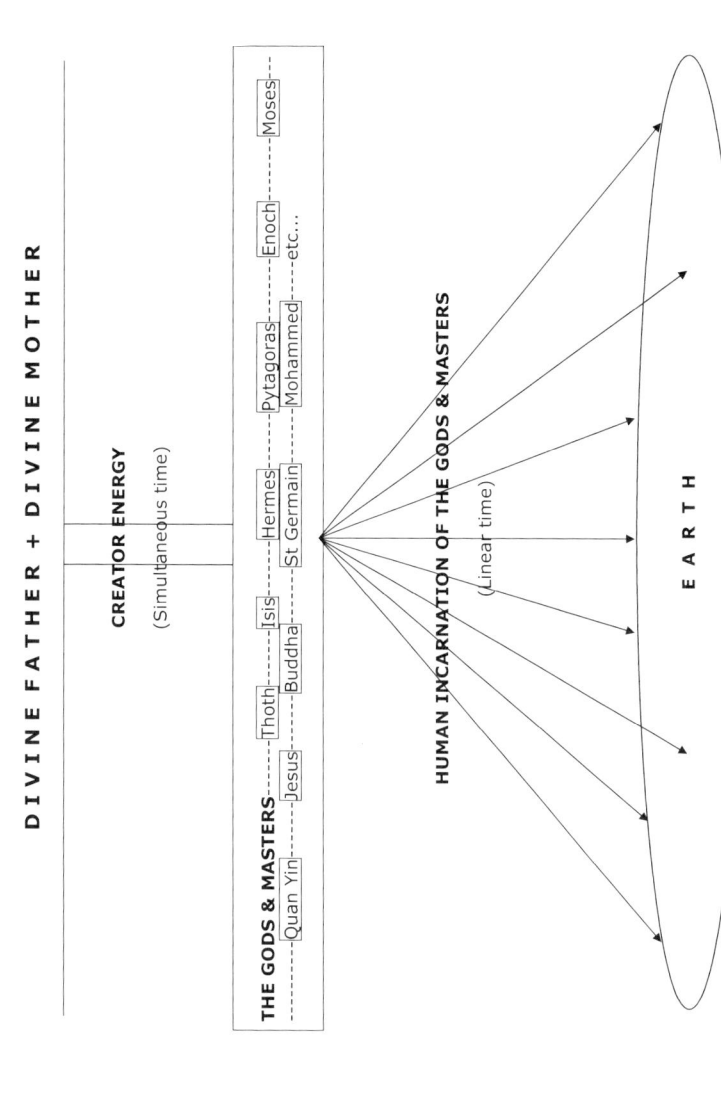

FIGURE 5: *The Divine Masters and Sons of God incarnations on earth are simultaneous embodiment of the same Creator Energy.*

"This completion and the coming together of all your manifested human Gods and Divine Masters is the relative understanding of what the Divine Creator is. The Masters become aware of their individual role and participation in this plan, but the actual fulfillment of this divine act - the alignment of earth with Creator Energy - happens at this moment in your earth history."

"Now, then, is the forthcoming emergence of the Masters and their divine allies, which will combine their energetic focus into one creative force, aligned with the divine Source. Through these incarnations and anchoring of Creator Energy, earth is now finally at the verge of becoming one again with the cosmos, as originally created by the thought of the Divine-Father and the Divine Mother of your planetary and galactic systems. "All are one" means all *is* one as well, because one can only manifest as eternity, but eternity can only be defined as one."

THE MASTERS' ROLE AND FUNCTIONING ...

"The particular role of the Divine Masters in embodying the frequency and expression of the Creator Energy is to provide the other participating beings with the necessary fuel they need to proceed. They are the operational power of this creator system now on earth. They are the fabric by which a new physical life can now exist through their remembrance and their own self-discovery. The fuel we speak of is the divine *love vibration* which carries all of life. By the thoughts and actions of love, the Masters fuel other beings, awakening and spreading the body / expression of the Divine Creator, as the Creator *is* love."

"Up to this day, the Masters carried enough of the Creator Energy particles so as to remember their state of origin as they walk the earth. Even though their role was brief or apparently temporary from a human perspective, they contributed enough information or energetic expression and vibration into this physical system so that their mission may come to the completion we speak of now. They carried and translated enough teachings and information so as to prepare others for the enormous magnitude and power of what is about to unfold in your physical reality. This new energy is divine love but also *divine truth*. And when you say divine truth, all the false barriers begin to fall to reveal this truth, which the Masters have already launched into being."

"Truth, however, is not experienced physically at first, but rather energetically. It is also related to the process of remembrance because the remembrance of your soul essence is and can only be truthful. When the Masters explore who they really are and achieve this crucial understanding, they realize that the energy with which they have merged is nothing but truth. So, by remembering and experiencing their true soul essence, they access and bring about the essence of truth in this reality, through their own physicality. And along with this remembrance and experience of the true self, the Masters' *thoughts* begin to affect and enhance the mind matrix of all humans. Their *love* affects and enhances the spiritual matrix of all humans. Their *word and expression* affect and enhance the creative matrix of all humans. Through this remembrance, the Masters realize that they *are* the human matrix and its potential. The Masters' mind affects all of humanity as if it were one and the same person, only dispersed in a few billion individuals. However, their work requires that they remain in their physical encasement in order to complete the anchoring process of Creator Energy on this earth plane."

HOW ARE ALL THE MASTERS RELATED? HOW CAN HUMANS ACHIEVE THIS LEVEL OF MASTERY? ...

"Each Master is his own being while working with the same frequency and formula that all the Masters carry with them in their physical life. They are of the same soul ancestry or lineage which means they are capable of transforming their being in physical form and other material forms and performing the same tasks that all Masters do. Due to their kindred soul connection, they are capable of experiencing the spirit vibration as well as the frequency of other

Masters while in physical form. Experiencing their vibration or frequency means that they have access to all that the Divine Masters are, all that they have ever been or will ever be. They have access to their memory cells and can experience these other Masters' being in a direct and complete way as they carry the same formula they all are made of."

"Indeed, everyone has the potential to experience their own soul lineage. Humans will experience the frequency that matches their personal and individual formula. While all souls are interconnected, each individual soul will ask and receive that which it needs in order to recognize its ancestry or lineage to its Divine Creator. Therefore, an individual in physical form may experience one entity or frequency in spirit form, which will represent their particular soul lineage. They may or may not experience the vibration of one particular Divine Master. Their personal experience of their soul lineage is relevant to their own spiritual development and will continue expanding and evolving until they are able to see themselves as one entity merged with their Divine Creator. The ultimate destination is not to see one's self matching another Divine Master's frequency. The ultimate destination or goal is to experience one's soul blended with the consciousness of the Creator. In this place, their soul lineage will appear as an inseparable particle of the Divine Creator, and will give them access to the full knowledge of who they really are."

"Furthermore, one may perceive the Divine Father in the human form of one Master such as Jesus or Buddha, for example, but they are, in fact, connecting to the *frequency range* of the Creator Energy this Master has embodied. It is imperative that you blend with an image that you *recognize*; otherwise you have no point of reference to describe what you are experiencing in human terms. While the Divine Father and Divine Mother are pure energy, there must be a way to describe *in the finite* what Creator Energy and Source Energy are, and that is through a *person* as well as an experience that is recognized and understood by the human mind."

EXPERIENCING HUMANNESS AMONG HUMANS ...

The Divine Father continues: "The Divine Masters are the ones embodying the Creator Energy frequency and vibration. They are my counterparts, so to speak, in the physical realm - an association of grand importance, no matter how much of a far-fetched concept it may appear to the material mind. The Masters are perceived as human but their spirit form is that of the divine, a different and unique formula, indeed."

"At times, the Masters realize that those whom they are amongst persist in reminding them of their humanness or weaknesses. Some will dissect every word they say and look for clues, issues or stumbling blocks to make them smaller, so that they feel at ease in the presence of a Master. Indeed, it is unfortunate but also part of the human experience. It is imperative that the Masters resemble humans although they may experience difficulty in feeling misunderstood or possibly blamed for not accepting the human mode of thinking which they perceive as trivial. There is no harm or concern in them feeling more evolved spiritually, intellectually, telekinetically and vibrationally, as they are! And that is because they embody an enormous frequency which is undetectable to the average humans - unless they begin to vibrate at that level. So, the Masters' challenge is to remain in their splendor, while accepting that they will be perceived according to the reality their interlocutor is accepting at the moment."

"Many Masters also dislike being human because they refuse to associate with the human way of feeling and processing emotions because they function entirely on different levels and frequencies. They must, however, reveal themselves as a human, while being truly a divine being. Their physical apparatus itself is the living formula of divinity. The rest, such as the work they do, is simply the framework within which they function in this world."

"The humanness a true Master enjoys is the sacredness and beauty of human life. The humanness others speak of is one that attaches you to mundane and unnecessary vibrations, leading to discomfort, self-sacrifice, self-blame and despair. That is a *human* perception of humanness which is not the Masters' reality. The Masters acknowledge the beauty of emotions as tools to experience who they truly are as a human, a personality and a being. That is a *divine* perception of that same humanness."

REASSEMBLING OTHER PARTICLES OF THE SELF ...

"As mentioned earlier, the Masters appear in one physical body, but they are part of another bigger body that shares the same formula. These other particles are distributed evenly throughout this sphere and beyond, in various shapes and forms: human, angelic and other non-material bodies. There are 1,100 particles of the same being altogether which form the Creator Energy. However, it is more accurate to say that this is the number for the *initial* emergence of these particles. At this moment in time, there are 3,300,000 individual beings, physical and non-physical, on earth and elsewhere, who are all an *aspect* of this Creator Energy in the past, present and future - a difficult concept to accept from your human perspective but nonetheless accurate from the spirit standpoint."

"Indeed, the Masters are of a divine nature, unique in the sense of their physicality. They are, in fact, in physical form. They are, in fact, experiencing physical life. However, they are not a physical being. They are simply assigning their focus to a physical reality in their awakened state. This means when their consciousness is not focused on their physicality, it is in existence in another medium referred to as spirit self. The spirit self expresses one life through a physical body, among many other expressions. Therefore, the Masters' physical body and physicality are merely one aspect of their entire consciousness. In fact, they are simultaneously expressing their consciousness of tremendous reach, in a multitude of beings currently in physical and non-physical form. This does not mean they are fragmented in many pieces. It simply means that their consciousness is able to express itself simultaneously in several physical manifestations, several particles or bodies at once."

"On the other hand, the other particles of the Masters' being are part of the self-realization process. The fact that they are dispersed does not make them difficult to reach. Those who counsel the Masters on their journey link them with the multitude of celestial, light or star beings who are simultaneously completing the same journey which is to anchor the Creator Energy and consciousness onto this plane. Therefore, many are on the same broadcast. What makes this communication special is that it is retrieved by the Masters' physical brain in a different way. Their understanding is somewhat different, as their genetic makeup allows them to receive and diffuse energy in a unique way. The broadcast and communications of the Creator Energy phenomenon are not a series of words or information. It is a *vibration* that is released to all of those who are able to receive it."

"To access this broadcast, the Masters and their particles must reach a brainwave frequency of 1MHz. therefore traverse many different frequencies in order to access the doorway to the Divine Father and these divine broadcasts. Not only can the Masters reach such tremendous levels of brain functioning, but they can sustain them, be focused on and discern several of these communications at once." (Figure 6 on page 57)

"The Masters accomplish such phenomenal task of attaining higher frequencies by training and re-programming their mind, a process which they, in turn, teach others. Once they master such process, the Masters must sustain these higher amounts of electrical energy throughout their earth career which can be 300 or 400 years."

DIVINE MIND	BRAINWAVE Frequency	BRAINWAVE Frequency	HUMAN MIND
Oneness with Creator-Father and Source Energy	1 MHz		
Access to Divine Father and Source Energy	500,000 to 1MHz		
Universal band	500,000 Hz		
Access to galactic band	100.000 Hz		
Spontaneous communication with invisible realms	1,000 to 1MHz		
Unconditional spontaneous healing	5,000 to 1MHz		
Human mind matrix / spiritual oneness	1000 Hz		
		130 Hz to 420 Hz	Planetary system orbit frequency
		100 to 500 Hz	Access to spontaneous healing and cell regeneration.
		35 to 45 Hz	High level learning
		13 to 17 Hz	Beta: "Normal" awakened / alert state
		7-12 Hz	Earth frequency
		8 to 12 Hz	Alpha: Light relaxation.
		3 to 7 Hz	Theta: Deep relaxation, Trance.
		1.0 to 3 Hz	Delta; Deep sleep. Lucid dream
		0.1 to 1.0 Hz	Mind stillness / Access to higher realms / Telepathic access
		0Hz	ZERO POINT FREQUENCY / Point of Transfer (from human to divine / time to timeless / finite to infinite)

Figure 6: This chart shows the frequencies to access the Divine Creator / Source Energy and experience many layers of reality: Human and Divine (1Hz = 1 cycle per second. 1MHz = 1 million cycles per second)

HOW CAN ONE LIVE 300 YEARS IN ONE PHYSICAL BODY? ...

"The Masters who are able to sustain a physical body for 300 or 400 years will choose to do so in order to complete their mission of anchoring the new energies on earth. What you are asking is how one may remain in one body for a few hundred years without disintegrating. The Masters are able to preserve their human faculties and return their body into its original state of divinity while in physical form because their chemical makeup is not equivocal with other humans. The transition from divinity to human and from human to divinity is the same. All they have to do is accept and acknowledge that light *is* their original state of being and that it cannot be contained in one physical body, nor can it be contained in one physical atmosphere. The dispersion and the recollection of their body particles that are found in many systems at once, allow the Masters to experience their non-physicality, thereby eliminate the limitations imposed by the human condition."

"Your question about how to maintain this one physical body for a prolonged period of time is an ordinary and natural quandary, coming from the perspective of your human expression. However, if looked at from the perspective of your spirit self, you will see that you can ultimately control the condition and fertility of your cells for a prolonged period of time by allowing your focus to remain only on the conditions of your physical body that you wish to keep. This does not require any supernatural powers. This only requires an awareness of who you are as a spirit being. It seems like a simplistic statement. However, when you begin to truly experience who you are as a spirit, you will realize that you are no longer attached to your physicality. Rather, you are able to be *outside* of it, control it and maintain the physicality you choose, for as long as you choose it. This awareness of self is nothing but the ultimate and permanent blending experience of the spirit self with the Creator Energy from which the Masters spring. If you are blended with and are an extension of Creator Energy, you are therefore capable of appearing in and controlling the physical body you wish to have. It is as if you were starting over, so to speak, from spirit form to physical form. Only you are doing so, not as an infant being born anew, but as an adult with the age and the appearance you wish to have."

"Indeed, it is the ultimate way of the Masters - to be born as a human infant, expand their consciousness to the point of remerging with the Creator Energy that created them, and return, so to speak, to the same physical body over and over without interruption. Although the spirit self is in existence outside the body under many circumstances such as the sleeping state, meditation and the dream state, this process of leaving and returning to the body is similar in the sense of mind focus. However, it is different in terms of control and energy manipulation. As a Master being, you are in the ultimate control of your spirit self, able to appear within and command the time-space continuum of your physicality. This mastery and control allow the Master to maintain a physical body of their choosing for as many years as they wish - 200, 300 or 400 years at a time."

HOW IS THE REALIZATION OF "WHO YOU ARE" RELATED TO WHAT WE CALL ASCENSION? ...

"Indeed, you have already realized that 'who you are' is the process of self-realization *and* ascension. They are one and the same. All are here to experience their own self-realization. However, to say that all humans or other physical beings are destined to accomplish their self-realization in the same way as the Masters is inconsistent with the fact that experience is subjective. It can be, however, a total possibility."

"While all those Masters have accomplished the same realization, they have chosen different ways to manifest physically and use these universal laws and tools to serve and fulfill their own destiny. That is, indeed, why they are called Divine Masters. They have recognized and experienced the merging of their spirit self with their Divine Creator while they remained in physical form. That *is* the process of self-realization and ascension all at once. At this juncture, however, the Master may choose to remain in spirit form or to continue manifesting his physicality for as many years as needed in the way I have described above. Ascension is, therefore, not a lifting process. Rather, it is a consciousness expansion process that allows a *merging* with the divine Creator Energy while still in physical form, and that is also precisely the total realization of "who you really are". (See figure 7 on page 61)

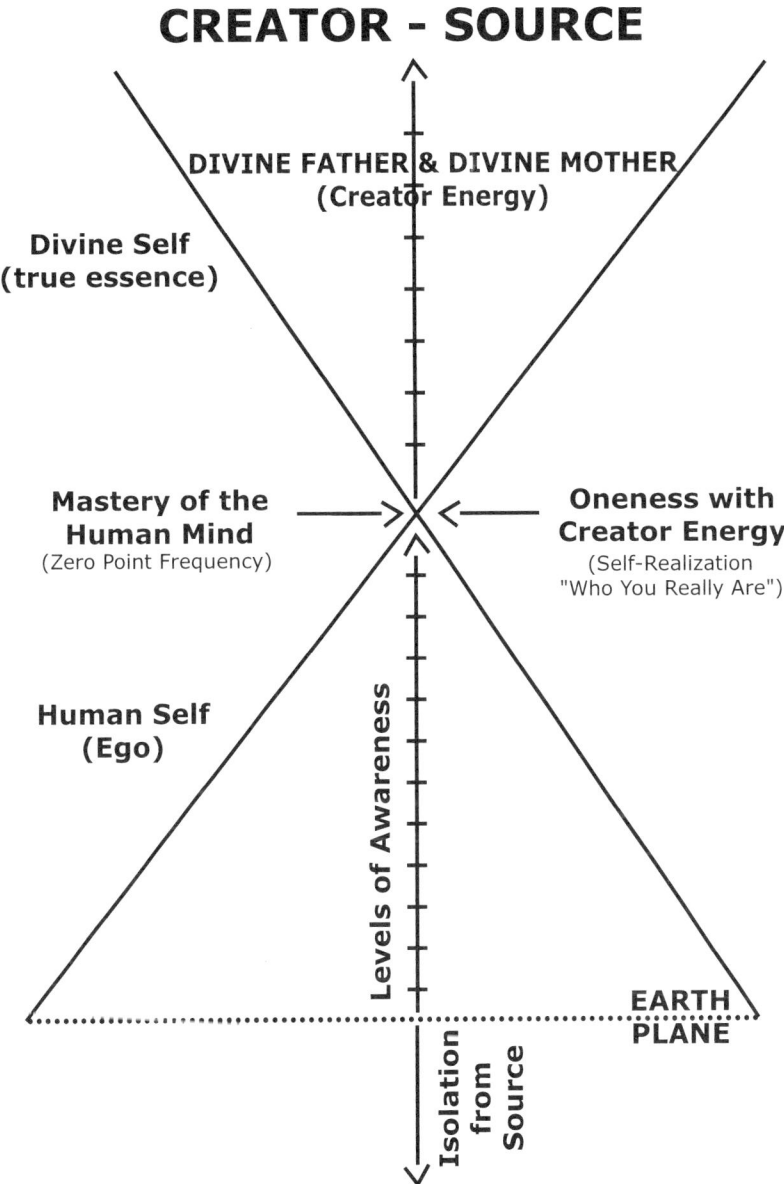

FIGURE 7: Self-realization and Ascension process

MERGING WITH THE DIVINE CREATOR IS ALSO REMEMBERING ...

"Merging with the Divine Creator is also remembering who you are and this reunification can only happen when the required energy fields and frequencies which allow such phenomenon to occur in the physical are present. *Full* remembrance is necessary when it is time for the Masters to depart from this plane. What they require first, however, is sufficient memory and perception that they are, in fact, who you are, so that they can proceed with their public and worldly actions in a conscious and deliberate manner."

"Many beings are awaiting such movement and alignment of energetics on earth which will trigger a sequence of activations of utmost significance. These movements are related to the symbiotic fields of your planet that will enhance clarity in portions of the physical brain, which can then enable the experience of merging and remembrance for everyone."

"Now is the time for such a happening, as the emerging Masters of your time can no longer sustain their current human existence. They have found all the clues to escape the human condition which no longer serves them. This means, they no longer require human emotions, programming or any of the human limitations and fears. They have become *fearless*, indeed, as the illusion of this human reality has become so obvious to them. They can now begin to reveal their true divine self and abilities to others with ease and collaborate freely and openly with the angelic and celestial realms while in the flesh. They will live in a human body as a divine being in full awareness of who they are and what they are here to accomplish. This is the process for all Masters who have come throughout your history and achieved the same type of remembrance and awakening to their own divine self."

ABOUT HUMAN EMOTIONS ...

"These changes and the remembrance process affect the Masters intellectually, as they absorb a tremendous amount of information in a minute amount of time. They learn to access anything at a blink of an eye, any subject of any proportion and in any layer of reality."

"Remembrance also affects them emotionally, as they see themselves as a child of heaven in pure positive energy form. The emotions that accompany such phenomena are nothing short of pure and divine love. The emotions that they normally experience when they commune with the Divine Father become constant. They are able to sustain this energy in their physical body because this is the arrangement for their physical manifestation."

"The Masters' remembrance and merging with the Divine Creator is also emotional because of the amount of love energy being focused on through this experience in which they now bathe permanently. It triggers a frequency on the level of emotions, which is unquestionably powerful. Their passion *is* emotional. Their love for goodness *is* emotional. Their entire physical body is an emotional sensory receptor of love and beauty. They are connected instantly to the realm of pure goodness."

HOW DOES ONE KNOW ONE HAS ARRIVED? WHAT IS THIS MERGING EXPERIENCE LIKE? ...

"We (the divine counselors speaking for the Divine Father) are hesitant to describe this experience in human terms, as it is a direct and spontaneous phenomenon, which occurs to each individual, as he / she begins to explore that expansion. Putting words to such an experience will limit the human mind in its own expansion, because it will tend to project and fabricate this experience as described by another. Therefore, it is best to say that the continuous expansion of consciousness allows a unique merging experience with the divine which, in turn, demonstrates who one really is. If one allows it, then it shall be."

"The Masters also *believe* they are the Creator Energy incarnate, so they experience life as if they were. All that they experience is from the perspective of a Creator. Their "proof" happens when they see and experience their real Divine Creator while in the flesh. The Masters understand and remember who they are, and, therefore, have no doubt about their ancestry or purpose. Their remembrance of who they are leads them to the proof they will no longer require."

REMEMBERING "WHO YOU ARE" IS NECESSARY FOR TOTAL HEALING AND TOTAL HEALING IS NECESSARY FOR REMEMBERING "WHO YOU ARE"...

"If you remember a particular event in your past consciousness, then you are able to locate its vibration and associate it with another frequency in order for it to heal. Just by remembering, you are extrapolating the frequencies that are buried under your physicality."

"The Masters are the healers of an entire generation, and all those suffering from the same physical ailments are healed through the askings of the Masters. All that affects the Masters, affects others. As they expand their consciousness and merge with the Divine Creator, they encompass all those frequencies between their human mind and their ultimate destination (the Divine Creator), and that includes the collective mind matrix. Therefore, while they bear no responsibility, it is necessary for them to ask for the things that benefit others as well as themselves. When or if they experience physical symptoms, this allows them to summon the cosmic healing reality for all. It is, in fact, in order for them to request the help of the governing agencies of the Source, who portray them as the "filter", so to speak, and begin the healing on a global scale."

"However, the Masters must also heal the old wounds affecting their own cerebral functioning that happen during the human incarnation process. The humanness that resides within them makes place for an enhanced perspective of the human condition. They must heal the wounds and heart-felt pains in order for them to relinquish this sort of humanness and replace it with another. Through this healing, they begin to see themselves entrenched with the light, as they were originally born on this planet, and will relinquish once and for all the aspect of humanness that attracts pain or suffering."

"This state - deep and complete healing - cannot be accomplished without the realization of who you are. Even though self-realization is as unique as the individual experiencing it, it has some attributes that all share. When the Divine Masters remember who they really are, they feel, hear and perceive everything as one indivisible entity, which is indescribable in human terms. This remembrance is on a cellular level, not on an intellectual one. The experience of unity with the Divine Creator is that of elation, an ecstatic vibration of love. When blended with the Divine Creator, the Masters experience no division, no separation. They feel only pure love. However, the process of remembering does not give them access to everything. It simply shows them who they are. Once they know who they are, then, *from that place of complete blending*, they begin to ask for the information, the knowledge or the healing that they need. They become the perfected vehicle of the light and will have access to total and complete healing when they remember who you truly are."

CAN THE HUMAN MIND ACHIEVE THIS STATE OF REMEMBRANCE AND BE TOTALLY FREE OF DISEASE, FEAR AND NEGATIVITY? ...

"Child of heaven, yes, indeed. The human mind can alter its perception of reality and be devoid of all disease, fear and negativity. The time has come when this realization becomes a normal factor in this physical life, when humans will no longer need fear to justify their weaknesses. They can resolve their daily quandaries by seeing this illusion - fear - as a temporary practice ground for self-discovery. This new focus will also give them access to the remembrance they seek."

"You may also be asking whether the human nature is able to explore both truth and illusion (fear or negativity) at once. The illusion falls within the human realm, not the divine, which means that it is your human mind that perceives the illusion through its sensory perception. The divine mind cannot perceive the illusion per se, as it is part of the human perceptual fields, not the divine!"

IN CONCLUSION ...

"Remembrance is the process of expanding your consciousness to higher layers of reality, which *is* the reassembly of all portions of your self, which *is* the process of merging with the Divine Creator, which *is* what you call ascension and that is also the total and complete experience of who you really are. Therefore, when you ask to know "who you really are", you launch a powerful mechanism of creation into the universe that will, in turn, generate a multitude of experiences encompassing all those described. The culmination and completion of these experiences *while in the flesh* is the work of the Masters - the imminent potential and destiny for all humans at this moment in earth's history and time."

4

The Original Home

As I asked about the geographical arrangement of the worlds, I began to see the universal organization of the different planetary and galactic systems, their approximate distance from earth and their overall feel and nature, as well as the beings that originate and dwell therein. I wondered where the Masters had originated prior to their physical incarnation and where they return once their mission is complete. The Assembly[33] explains below:

◆ ◆ ◆

"The physical universes are organized in such a way as to perpetually gravitate around a nucleus called the *Central Suns*[34], which supports and feeds the respective planets and systems. Earth belongs to the 99th of the 100,000[35] universes, all revolving around the *Central Universe*[36] which, in turn, attaches you to the Creator-Source. And since each universe consists of billions of galaxies, within which are billions of planetary and solar systems, the distance between your

---

33 Assembly: Spirit Family of the Masters perpetually attached to their energy and mission.
34 Central Suns: Area in the center of each universe that controls and feeds life energy within all surrounding galaxies, planetary and star systems.
35 100,000 universes: The approximate number of universes surrounding earth. This number is continuously augmenting as creation is infinitely on-going.
36 Central Universe: Core universe that controls and feeds thousand of surrounding universes.

planet and the Central Universe exceeds 100 billion light years." (See figure 8 on page 69)

"Most humans belong to your local planetary or galactic systems. However, a great number of beings currently in human form are original residents of other universes billions of light-years away from earth. They co-exist on earth and time-travel between universes continuously. The way to travel such great distances is through consciousness projection and through the use of energy grids. The more evolved a consciousness is, the faster and farther it can travel. There is a way to travel instantly from one system to another and from one universe to the next. However, such is the work of the more highly evolved beings into which humans are gradually transmuting."

"When a being originating from a different universe appears in your local system in human form, this being must first break down its energetic components so as to fit in a new physical system. Spirit groups[37] and families from evolved universes travel together and typically land in proximity of their final destination. Some will then materialize in human form and find each other as family members or in other close relationships, while others remain in spirit form but continue to be energetically attached to their counterparts in physical form."

---

37   Spirit groups: Soul groups or spirit family.

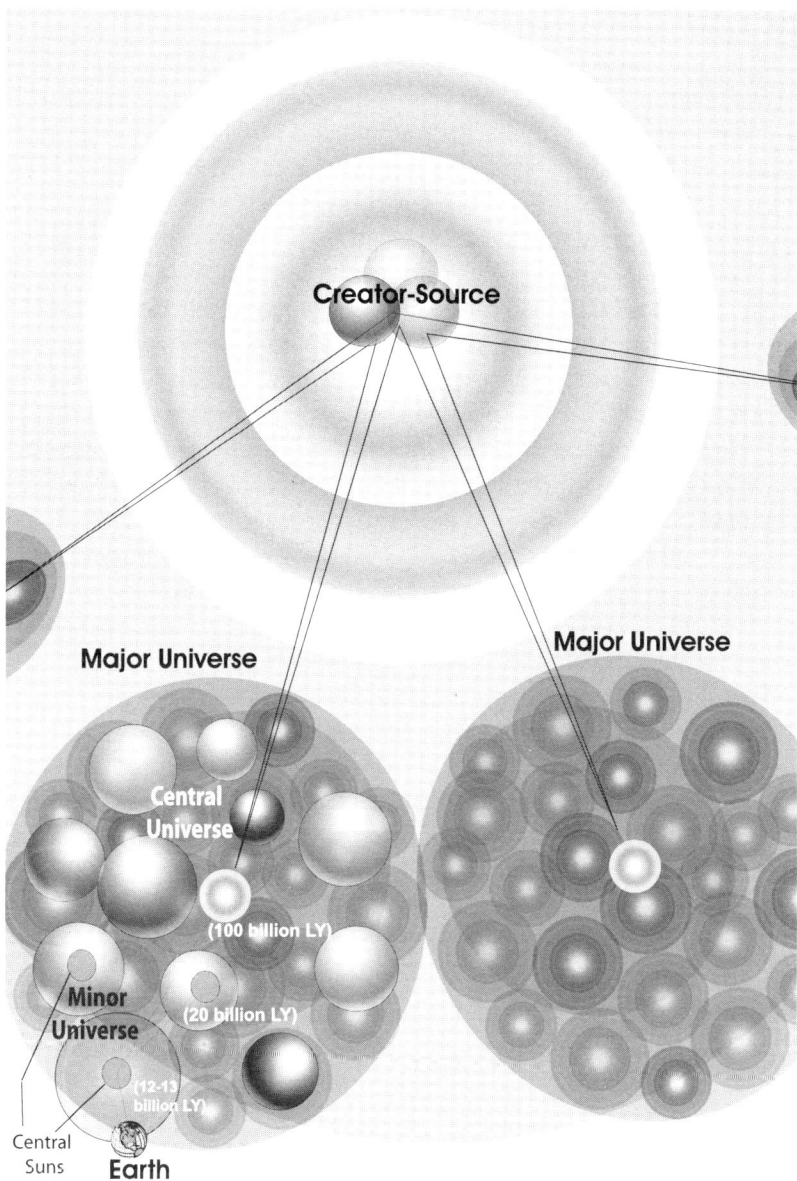

FIGURE 8: Universal organization in relation to the Creator-Source

THE CENTRAL UNIVERSE ...

"The Divine Masters originate in the *Central Universe* or the *First Universe*[38], around which all other universes revolve. (Refer to figure 8 on page 69) This universe is the nucleus or core land from which the energy that supports life on all surrounding universes and planetary systems springs. It is the most massive territory as it must sustain the birth, control, management and proliferation of over 100,000 universes. This massive land also produces the suns of all the surrounding universes and, in turn, creates a gravitational area for each universe, the area of the *Central Suns*."

"The Central Universe is primarily the 'governmental' headquarter of the surrounding worlds, as it holds the administrative body managing the created worlds. It is responsible for maintaining the appropriate energy proliferation, which must always be one with Source. When or if great destructive energy overtakes a planetary system, it is the administrative body of the Central Universe that organizes the dispensation of the appropriate beings and missions to restore oneness within the cosmic structure of the surrounding worlds."

"This Central Universe allows all others to breathe, so to speak, and feeds them the appropriate energy patterns in order to sustain life in a variety of ways. The Central Universe, in which the Divine Masters dwell, is also recognized as the nucleus or core universe of all surrounding universes, due to the fact that it distributes all spiritual, "mind-al" and physical functioning and establishes the nature of the beings within each."

"Within the Central Universe are several million 'soldiers' (not to be confused with your concept of soldier, as in an army). These soldiers are the guardians of this territory as they extrapolate information from their various posts and surrender them to the appropriate agencies that maintain perpetual energetic balance within the various universes."

"There is much to describe in terms of differences between the Central Universe and the universes surrounding it. One is the size of its planets that are 7 to 10 times larger than your earth, with an atmosphere that is constant and more or less invariable. As such, the beings dwelling in these locations are *light beings* that exist within

---
38 First Universe: Central Universe.

this atmosphere without physical bodies. They possess a form that does not need to materialize or receive physical 'nourishment' in order to be sustained."

"The entire structure of the planets within the Central Universe is similar to an energy form which is crystal-like. The core planet of this universe possesses an atmosphere which appears as a light blue haze with mostly pinkish skies. The environment feels like an everlasting dusk, perpetually bathed in great calm, beauty and dignity. The inhabitants of the Central Universe are all loving and wise."

"The Divine Masters begin life on the core planet of the Central Universe and observe this arrangement throughout their careers, unless called to assist a planet in need such as your earth. This location is their usual dwelling place. They reside in a domain that can be compared to a 'castle' of glass or crystal-like material. The castle sits on endless grounds and the scenery goes on infinitely. It is beautifully distributed and is surrounded by immense gardens. There are *artists-beings* working in the gardens and they maneuver energy in such a way as to create what looks like plant life of breathtaking beauty. Compared to plants on earth, these may look like giant flowers, about 6 or 7 feet tall, carrying a life force unknown on earth. Their colors vary, but they are mostly close to what you call pink. Their texture appears like a soft plastic of some sort which is durable and flexible."

"One most spectacular aspect of this central planet is its massive *sea of glass*, an area that can be compared to your stadiums, only about 70 times larger, where intra-universal and inter-galactic communications occur. Communication on these worlds is not accomplished through language or even symbols. It is achieved through *energetic reflectivity*[39]. Reflectivity is the process by which the energy field from one area or planet blasts its news and information onto another, which then refracts and reflects onto a surface - the sea of glass - in such a way as to be automatically and spontaneously understood by any type of being from any given universe. The energetic reflectivity process is facilitated and maneuvered by the Power Controllers[40] through the use of grids that distribute information evenly in and out of the worlds. Once landed on the sea of glass surface, all beings, regardless of their origin or location, are able to assimilate

---

39 Reflectivity: Process by which energetic information is transferred from one point to another.
40 Power Controllers: Beings in spirit form responsible for maneuvering energy.

the significance of the material being shown. Your earth's history, for example, has been projected onto this spectacular surface for millennia at a time and countless beings from far-flung universes have followed carefully the main shifts and tremendous events of your planet since its original conception. Indeed, it is a most splendid phenomenon which will soon be discovered within your sphere allowing you, the inhabitants of this earth, to regain your much anticipated trans-universal citizenship."

OTHER UNIVERSES ...

"Your earth belongs to a solar system and the *current* closest star to your system is about 4.2 light years away or approximately 23 trillion miles. The closest galaxy is more than 100,000 light years away or approximately 580,000 trillion miles, while the core of the closest universe is located more than 20 billion light years away or approximately 100 billion trillion miles. (See Figures 9 and 10 on pages 73 and 74) This tremendous space between the planetary systems and neighboring universes is partially responsible for the inability to translate into a comprehensible language their nature and functioning. Additionally, the life patterns as created and understood within these worlds is not only different but also inexplicable to the human mind until it is experienced directly through consciousness expansion. It is also impossible to accurately and fairly depict the nature and functioning of other surrounding planetary systems - let alone 100,000 universes! - within the scope of one book. Therefore, we shall attempt to describe the role and functioning of the worlds that are relevant to the current human destiny and evolution."

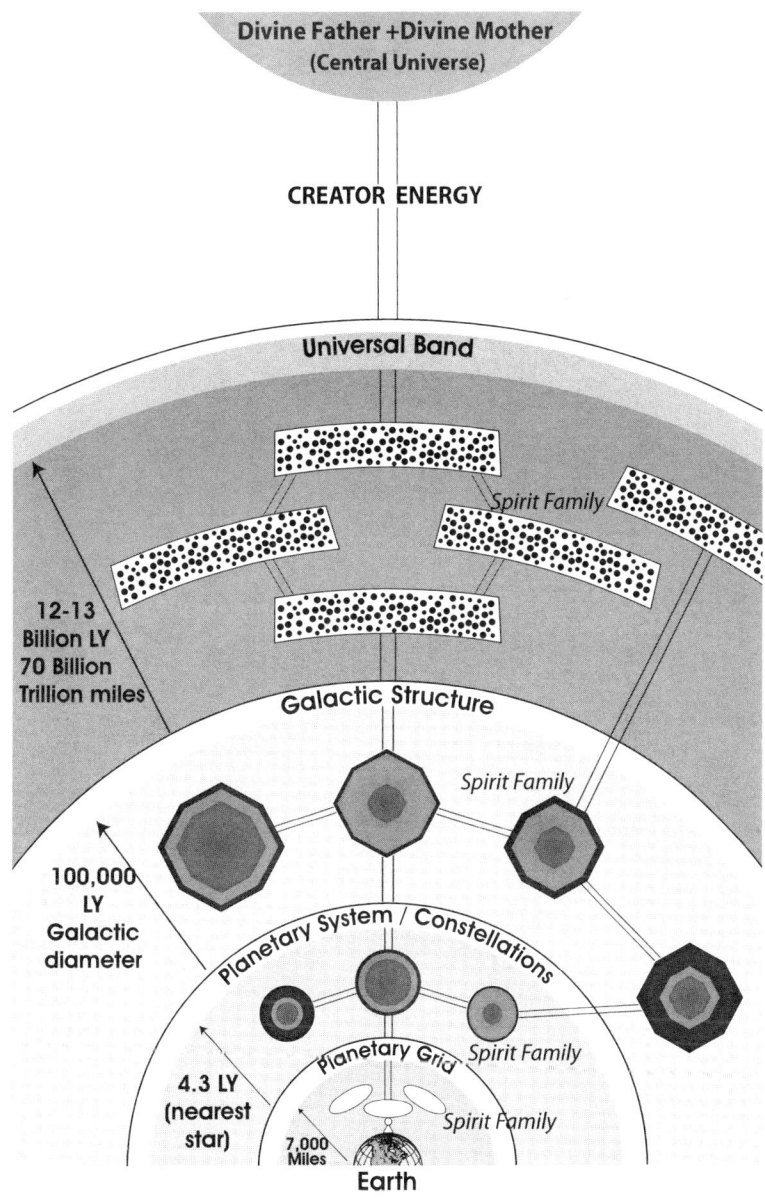

FIGURE 9: Distance between Earth, the Milky Way and the universal band

74 GOD Among Us: Inside the Mind of the Divine Masters

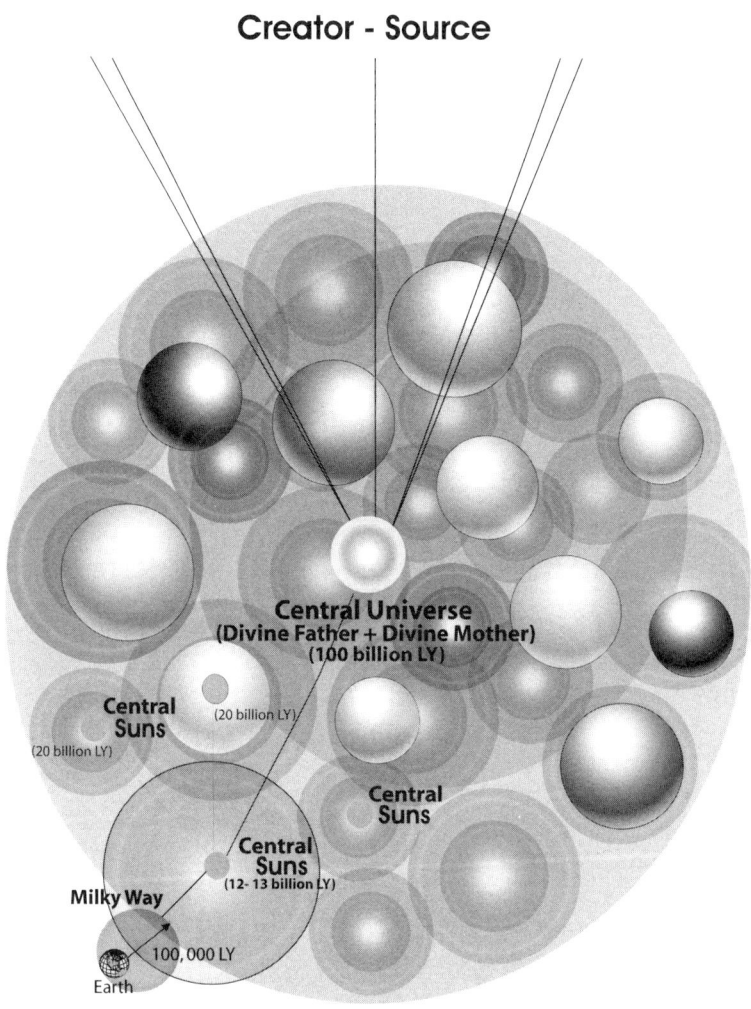

FIGURE 10: *Relationship and distance between Earth, the Central Suns and the Central Universe*

THE 7ᵀᴴ UNIVERSE ...

"The planets of this universe are of an extremely fiery nature. The atmosphere appears tremendously hot with colors ranging from what you would refer to as deep red to a blazing orange. The ground is rocky and mountainous."

"In this universe dwell the *Master Teachers*, those who elevate the human mind to its most current and appropriate level of evolution. Those Master Teachers can mastermind a tremendous plan of action, so to speak, and introduce new information, technology and spiritual insight to the human mind. Typically, these beings travel to the earthly plane but do not materialize. They work with humans through inspiration and, more importantly, during the sleep state when they are able to communicate new information in an accurate manner. When you awaken, you then retrieve this knowledge from what you call imagination, insight or inspiration. Global political or scientific breakthroughs, such as the discovery of electricity, computers or the original formulation of the governmental democratic constitutions, are all examples of the work and transmissions of these magnificent Master Teachers."

THE 4ᵀᴴ UNIVERSE ...

"Planets within this universe can be compared to airy space, with thin atmospheres and cloud-like formations in the skies. There are spirit and material beings on this plane. The physical beings that exist in these worlds are non-breathers, which means they do not have a respiratory system per se, but they can sustain life and the exchange of energy through their skin."

"In this universe dwell the *Angel Spirits* that are assigned to human destiny. They train and prepare in these territories for their mission to assist evolutionary beings such as humans. These Angel Spirits travel to your world when they have completely understood their own nature and role within your reality. They assist you by offering guidance on daily issues or predicaments, sorting out your desires and helping you progress on your spiritual journey. The Angel Spirits typically work in pairs and will continue to be the easier types of beings that humans can perceive. They deliver messages and information to guard you against harm or destruction."

THE 16TH UNIVERSE ...

"The 16th Universe exists in proximity of the 1st universe and is instrumental in communication procedures. It allows proper distribution of information and news broadcasts between the worlds and within each universe. The 16th universe may be compared to a nuclear power plant from which energy is distributed appropriately to different regions - The power grids that support the infrastructure of communication and exchange are stationed here. Consequently, the physical nature of the planets within this universe is mostly made of hard metals unknown on earth but that resemble titanium combined with silver. The energy of these metals supports a tremendous amount of information pouring in from the thousand universes and their respective planetary systems and blasting out to the various points of the far-flung space. The 16th Universe is the power center of a gigantic universal structure, with unfathomable power that exceeds your imagination. The beings that operate or manage this universe are the *Power Controllers*. However, the beings in charge of broadcasting and relaying information from one world to another are the *Translators* or *Interpreters*. These beings are responsible for collecting information from one world, then translating it into a language that may be comprehended by another. We are not referring to human languages, such as English or French. Rather, we are speaking of information contained within an energy field or frequency, such as sound or light, which needs to become compatible with the atmospheric restrictions and frequency range of another world in order for it to be deciphered. There is a great amount of information traveling to the earth plane that remains undetected and unnoticed by you. It is the work of these Power Controllers and Interpreters that allows the transportation and translation of information from other universes to become comprehensible to the human mind. Currently, there are thousands such beings roaming your planet and allowing greater cosmic information to become comprehensible to you. They work in conjunction with the Master Teachers who train the human mind and prepare it to receive such information in a clear and beneficial manner."

THE 28TH UNIVERSE ...

"This universe organizes the life patterns of evolutionary beings and allows the dispensation of new species that can be sustained in a given world. It is the place where new life patterns are created and integrated within previous ones, so as to continue expanding and feeding the evolutionary process of physical beings. In this universe dwell the *Life Designers* responsible for exploring new and different patterns of life - namely the physical formula through which a new species may be born. Your DNA is created by these Life Designers and its updated version continues to be introduced within your realm. While these beings are responsible for instilling new life patterns on a planet, it is the Divine Father and the Divine Mother that produce the spirit energy into form, so as to become integrated within the life formula. Therefore, you are the result of an 'engineered' physical formula in conjunction with the spirit energy of the Divine Father and Divine Mother."

THE 17TH UNIVERSE ...

"The 17th universe is the universe in which the *Universal Architects* dwell. These beings are in charge of creating a design for harmony and balance within each universe and planet. The Universal Architects formulate a creative and most appropriate 'setting' for the different species inhabiting the various planets. If it is required that a certain type of being inhabit a planet, the Universal Architects will creatively organize its patterns to accommodate harmonious work, play or worship opportunities. For example, the distribution of oceans and mountains on your planet provide propitious balance for such human expression and expansion. The Universal Architects work in conjunction with the Power Controllers, since the allocation of proper power structures must accompany the appropriate creative design of the planet."

THE 10TH AND THE 19TH UNIVERSES ...

"Both these universes are maintained for the overflow, so to speak, of other expanding universes. If a certain planet becomes inhabitable due to the formation of excessive nebulae, these worlds become replicas of the previously inhabited ones and will provide the necessary elements to transpose life from one universe to the other. It is imminent on your journey as a human being to realize that inter-galactic and trans-universal transport is not only possible but necessary for all evolutionary species. You will soon be approaching such a time, reason for which this information is provided."

THE 12TH AND THE 26TH UNIVERSES ...

"These 2 universes are irreversible, in the sense that they stabilize the distribution of gravity among the different worlds. While the Central Universe is responsible for maintaining gravitational forces throughout the multi-layered universes, it is assisted and supported by these 2 powerful areas of stability and control. The 12th and 26th universes are governed by the *Gravity Controllers* who also work in conjunction with the Power Controllers and other celestial forces."

THE 3ʳᵈ AND THE 5ᵗʰ UNIVERSES ...

"In these universes dwell the *Universal Builders* responsible for the organic and material building of the worlds. They assist in the planning, layout and distribution of the materials on a new world to maintain their atomic and chemical balance. These beings work in conjunction with the Universal Designers and Architects and assist in creating the substances that will support the overall patterns of the new world. They are responsible for the balance of atomic elements of your earth and are currently involved in restoring the chemical and material damages incurred by the human misuse of technology and misguided deeds.

THE 57ᵗʰ UNIVERSE ...

"This universe exists within proximity of your universe. However, due to the different patterns of life established there, it is almost impossible to describe its nature and functioning in a way or language that may be comprehended by the human mind. You do, however, exchange energetic information in the sense of creativity. Art and creative design as experienced on your earth is the result of energetic exchange with this 57ᵗʰ universe."

5

The Original Spirit Family

The original Spirit Family is the one to which every being is linked since its original creation or conception. We are created through the thought of the Divine Creator, along with other beings that share similar characteristics. Within the myriad creation of beings, no two creations are alike. However, some will share a similar formula thereby becoming part of one same soul group or Spirit Family. Additionally, these spirit groups differ not only in composition or genetic make-up, but also in nature and functioning.

The Divine Masters belong to the Spirit Family closest to the Divine Creator or, from a human perspective, the oldest. They carry a genetic encoding of the Creator-Energy that allows them to create universes and worlds - physical and non-physical - through the focused action of their mind. When in human or other material form, they travel from universe to universe and from one galaxy to another, accompanied by members of their original Spirit Family, who remain in spirit form and assist them on their physical journey. However, through their expeditions - regardless of the system in which they appear - the Masters will remain closely attached to the energy of the Divine Creator which is the very design of their nature and purpose. Evolutionary beings are no different in that respect as they too travel in spirit from system to system and remain attached energetically to their Spirit Family while they appear on earth in material form.

The following are communications between the Divine Masters and different members of their original Spirit Family. While the names of these beings may differ from Master to Master, their respective nature and role of teacher, guide or translator is identical.

◆   ◆   ◆

HOW IS COMMUNICATION WITH THE SPIRIT FAMILY ACHIEVED? ...

The Spirit Family explains: "The process by which the Masters and we communicate in this elaborate manner is by communing *live*, which means we hear their voice as they are transmitting their information and they also hear us. These conversations are telepathic in nature. Their physical body emits a certain amount of electromagnetic charge, which can then signal us in space that they are requiring information. Since we are connected energetically, vibrationally and through our lineage, we receive their request immediately and can respond to them. The only difference between these conversations and telepathy between human or other spirit beings is that these conversations require the Masters to sustain an energy that exceeds the normal human brain capacity. This means it is impossible for a typical human to receive this amount of energetic transmission in one sentence. Therefore, the Masters are connected to a circuit or grid that allows this sort of communication to occur with them and others that are simultaneously listening in on this broadcast. These others that are of the same mental charge as the Masters are all aspects of the same Creator Energy they represent."

"We are all dispersed within the Milky Way and farther away into space and within the Central Universe. We come to the Masters with information that they may need or request in a matter of seconds, even though the physical distance between their geographical location and the Central Universe is billions and billions of light years. It is an intricate process to sustain the massiveness of the Source's circuit and frequency and receive it within the physical realms instantaneously."

"The Masters, then, replicate the energetic information they receive from Source and translate it into words for the people of this earth. This truth is now being told simultaneously to all those emerging vehicles with similar vibration, as they are beginning to recognize their impact on the spiritual development of humanity. The Masters must, however, *ask* and receive the answer from their Divine Creator and guardians, for that is their agreement and universal law."

"On a physical level, all that is required of the Masters is to tune in. Tuning in means directing their focus and attention to the frequency that allows them to hear us. This frequency resides physically in the soul body, the 3 most outer layers of the energy field. In this invisible portion of the energy field, their vibrational rate reaches 734Hz, which is the *minimum* frequency required to begin communicating with the spirit world." (See figure 11 page 85)

"The physical brain of the Masters also is fashioned in such a way as to sustain an enormous amount of energy. It is capable of holding a brain wave frequency of 1MHz without incurring harm, as their brain is composed of a set of frequencies that cannot be found in the 'normal' human genetic make-up. In scientific terms, the genomes that make up their physical being are created from a formula that cannot be explained in human terms. (Refer to figure 6 on page 57) These frequencies, however, allow them to receive and understand clearly our communication and, in turn, diffuse this information in words others can comprehend.

THE ORIGINAL SPIRIT FAMILY: THE ASSEMBLY ...

The Masters' Spirit Family consists of a sacred *Assembly*, originating at the Creator-Source, which works with them consistently since their emergence in physical form on this planet. They are attached through the same energetic umbilical cord which, in turn, connects them to the Divine Father and Divine Mother in the Central Universe. (See figure 12 on page 86)

The Assembly explains: "The Masters and we, an Assembly of heavenly beings, have originated at the Creator-Source and have multiplied our energies more than a billion-fold in order to reach our far-flung material beings. While we may appear in any form of creation we wish and any universe we choose, we maintain at all times the frequency with which we are born - that of the Creator-Source, our only one and original creator frequency, also recognized as Love, Beauty, Goodness and Truth."

"By multiplying our energies into millions of different expressions, we are explicitly transmuting one frequency into another and creating worlds upon worlds. The Masters on earth are one of us, a group of beings at the origin of many, many creations. Together, we are responsible for the well-being of various planetary systems at once. Our 'names' can be revealed only to give you a sort of reference point as we do not possess English sounding names! We are, nonetheless, entities of heavenly nature assisting the Masters in their divine mission. When their mission is completed, they most certainly ascend back to where they originated - the abode of the Divine Father and Divine Mother whom they well know."

"The Assembly is also Creator Energy, the energy of the Divine Creator. It is comprised of 70 million or more individual entities, but we can only be perceived as 7 beings - or 8, if you count the Master in physical form. The brain capacity of the Masters allows them to maintain a frequency of 1MHz without incurring damage to their physicality. This frequency is the way by which they are able to tune into our wave length directly and deliberately." (Refer to figure 6 on page 57)

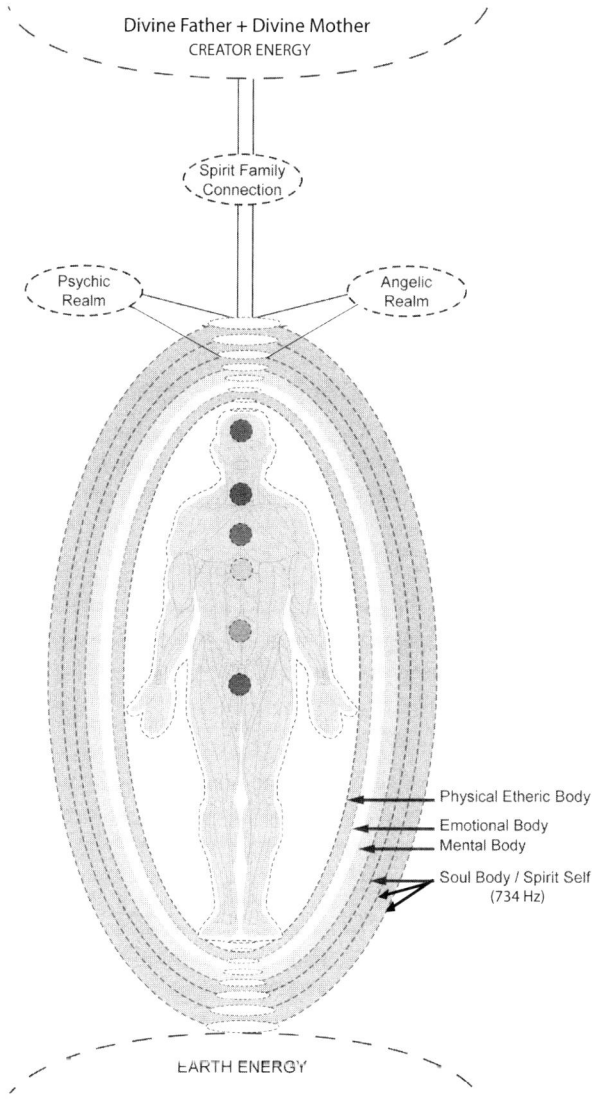

FIGURE 11: *The human energy field and its connection to the Spirit Family and higher realms*

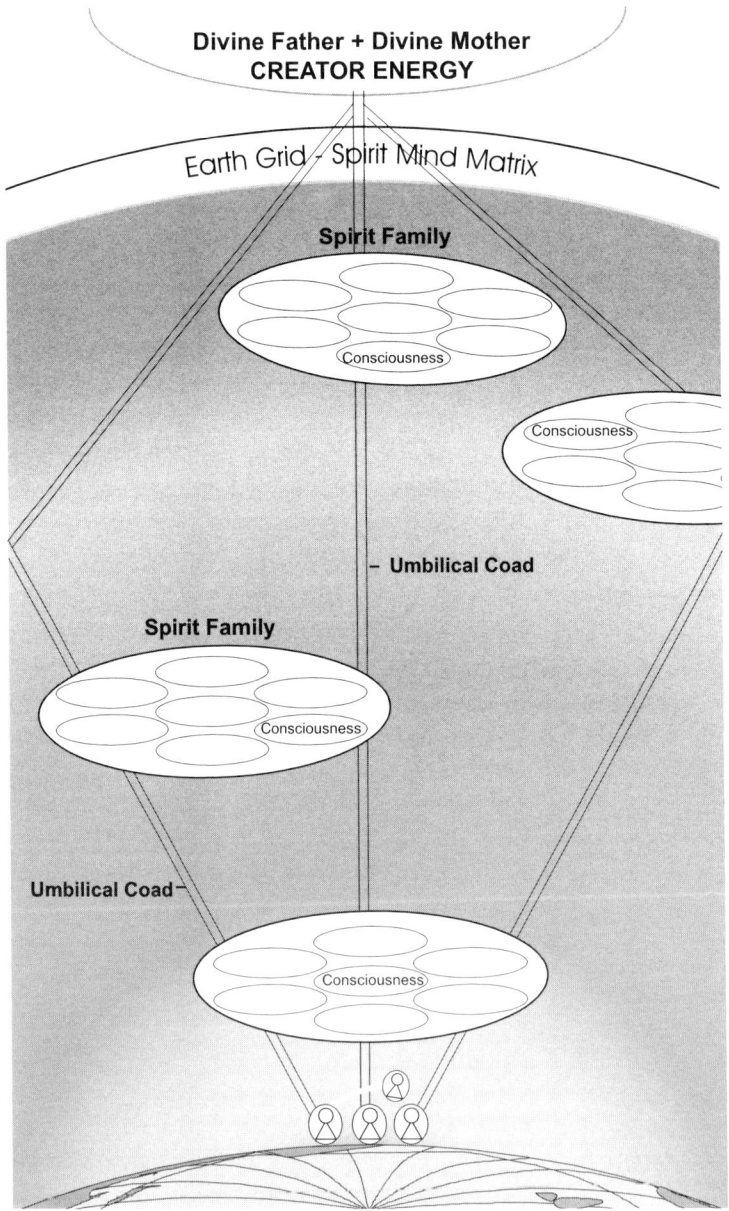

FIGURE 12: Spirit Family connection through the energetic umbilical cord

"The family members of the Masters embody the sacred formula of life and, together with the Masters, they form one entity - a Creator Energy so vast that it is unconceivable from a human perspective. However, the Masters and their Spirit Family are one. What makes them a Divine Master is that they recognize themselves as this Creator Energy of which we are speaking, *while they remain in their very material body*. Indeed, through this recognition of their own soul lineage, they are able to bring this truth to others, thereby becoming the creative fuel of humankind, all of which must and will be done through and by the Divine Masters and those attached to the Creator Energy."

"The Masters are able to perceive their Spirit Family, invisible guardians as well as the other invisible portions of themselves. We speak to them directly. It is an unbroken communion. It is the divine will that they experience human life multi-dimensionally, so that they may reveal it to others. It is imperative that they see, hear and perceive us effortlessly."

"We are here to assist them in the manipulation of energy fields and any endeavor they wish to pursue, for their divinity must eventually be expressed with no restrictions. By our mere presence in this planetary system, the Masters and we literally sustain millions of human lives into a frequency, a system of patterns and programming, that will allow the new shift. We deliver those materials and tools that the Masters require and reference to in order to proceed with such interactions."

"We may remain anonymous to others for awhile, until the Masters choose to elaborate further on their own origin. Indeed, they cannot explain us without explaining themselves, as we are one and same Creator Energy. Realization of who they are must be complete in order for them to proceed more cautiously about the delivery of their message. By cautiously, we mean a more precise and deliberate way of acting and expressing their true divine self. We understand the time frame within which they work, even if we are timeless. We also recognize the parameters of their physical reality. Otherwise, we cannot assist them properly."

"The Masters perceive us as a reflection of their own self, in so far as we are their Spirit Family. We have the same patterns and were created equally within the same frequency and vibration and out of the same fabric or energy form. As manipulators of energy, we are here to assist them, and we need their physicality to reach physical beings, while they need our invisible form to facilitate the energetic shifts of humanity. We are one entity - yet we have dispersed to over a thousand locales to form a tremendous circuit of information that carries the quality and attributes of Creator Energy."

"The Masters and we are the significant shift now being observed within the human realm. Our formula is not similar or comparable to that of humans. The Masters do carry the human DNA, which they need in order to appear in human form. However, this fact does not make them of the same human species. This difference is - in actuality - no difference, because one is an expansion of the other as the human genome will, in fact, be replaced by the one the Masters - and others - are representing now. Their divinity in the flesh is an *example* to where and how humans will evolve. That is the purpose of their existence within the human realm as well as the existence of all those recognizing their own divinity within them."

"When we say we are an extension of the Masters, it does not mean we are one being only. They and we form one consciousness, or one being. However, we also are individual consciousness within the larger Spirit Family consciousness. The other members are spirit guides that assist the Masters on their journey by acting as thought 'translators' allowing them to simply and purely channel the true and only Source Energy poured directly from the Creator of this system, which is the Source of Life, Love, Wisdom and Truth for this reality and others."

THE DIVINE CREATOR: THE DIVINE FATHER AND DIVINE MOTHER ...

"We shall attempt to describe the experience of the Divine Creator, although He is experienced somewhat differently by each individual being in material form. The Divine Creator encompasses both individual beings: the Divine Father and Divine Mother. Together, They are the divine beings responsible for creating the Central Universe, the surrounding universes and all physical and non-physical inhabitants therein. Your direct Creator is therefore called the *Divine Creator* who is also the combination of both beings: the *Divine Father* and *Divine Mother*."

"While the Masters may perceive the Divine Creator as a masculine or feminine energy, He has no gender per se - He is both masculine and feminine. The physical brain of the Masters, however, may identify this magnificent being as a masculine or feminine energy, because that aspect is what complements the nature and functioning of their own physicality at that moment in time or in one particular incarnation."

"The word *Father* or *Mother* comes spontaneously as the Masters experience Their energy directly. This experience comes through a merging process that occurs, at first, during a trance or meditative state, attained when their physical brain is sustained at *zero point frequency*[41] or 0Hz for at least 14 seconds. This state of mind quietude prevents interference from the normal human brain activity of the awakened state. This absolute mind stillness is necessary because anytime the human or conscious mind is activated, it is functioning through the *human* spectrum and therefore accessing knowledge *through that channel*. Zero point frequency is the *transfer point* or doorway leading from the human to the divine realms. (Refer to figure 6 on page 57) Similarly, it is also the passageway from time to timelessness and from finite to infinite.

As this merging with the Divine Creator occurs, it is remembered and becomes permanently ingrained in the conscious portion of the brain, so that the Masters may access it again spontaneously. At the same time, the physical body's vibrational rate is also raised, through breath, to approximately 1000 Hz or higher, which allows the conscious merging with the soul body or spirit self portion of the self. The quieting of the brain's activity to zero point and the raising of the body's vibration are the factors allowing a clear passage to the divine realms and the perfect merging with the Divine Father / Divine Mother frequency."

"When this state is achieved, a brilliant image may appear about 10 feet from the Masters' physical body (in the outer layer of their energy field) and create a powerful beam of light connecting them to it. The image may appear as the face or silhouette of a divine be-

---

41 Zero point frequency: Absence of vibration which is the bridge between the human / finite experience and the divine / infinite experience.

ing they recognize, possibly resembling a human Master they know. However, the energy they experience is the larger *consciousness* itself, from which that human Master has sprung."

"The Masters may hear or sense the words 'Father' or 'Mother', but the energy that accompanies these words - as well as the entire experience - is simply and clearly powerful, overly emotional and truthful. They do not only understand the words, but truly experience the relationship and meaning of the word 'Father' or 'Mother' at that very moment. The Father / Mother concept or Father / Mother figure, as experienced on earth, is that of a parent or guardian. However, in this context, Father / Mother is also Creator because they see and experience themselves as a true essence emerging directly from this brilliant and divine being. It is an energy altogether beyond physicality. It is them, as a soul particle of another greater one that is totally pure, absolutely real and utterly exquisite, all at once."

"Once they succeed in perceiving the Divine Creator, the image, the energy and the relationship of this Person remain attached to their being like a permanent seal as they go about experiencing physical life or exploring the unseen worlds. The Divine Creator becomes their direct link to Source. He is the One the Masters will hear, the One they will experience and commune with and, most of all, the One they will represent in this physical reality. There is no separation between His being and theirs, as they become Him in the physical, and He is them in the higher realms."

"The Masters also realize that this Creator Being and Force is not only their own experience, but that of many. What we mean is that the Divine Creator that they experience is the Creator of all humans and other material beings. He is the amalgamation of all consciousness at once and the creative force behind their reality. He is the energy from which they have sprung, along with their planetary systems, galaxies and surrounding universes. He is the Creator - the one and only representation and replica of Source. Merging with Him *is* merging with Source."

"The Divine Father / Mother address the Master: 'You are my first child of heaven and, subsequently, all humanity is as well, since you encompass the entire human matrix of thoughts. I am the Creator and the Source Energy. I am the Life in physical form as transmuted by you and through you. I am the breath of Life on earth and beyond. I am the Love energy - at the very least, the one which humans know.'"

"The Divine Creator is the replica of the expression / body of the Creator-Source, which means He is the direct link to the one and only Creator-Source. The Masters are here now on earth in place of Him. He sends the Masters to explore human life and redistribute misaligned energy within the universes appropriately. The Masters do this work simply by emerging in human form. The process is difficult in terms of breaking down their original formula into one that is compatible with physicality, thus the fragmentation of their memory cells, which must then be gradually reassembled. The retrieving of their information happens only because of the unbreakable link with the Divine Creator."

"Therefore, per their pre-natal arrangement, The Masters are able to consciously and directly communicate and experience the Divine Creator in a clear and focused manner. However, due to the remoteness of His physical location, which exceeds 100 billion light-years, they may also commune through other types of beings and translators that exist and work in different frequencies and physical locations, enabling a clear and uninterrupted flow of information. The beings responsible for breaking down information from such remote locations into a human language they can comprehend - and, in turn, express - are what we have been referring to as the Spirit Family. They are comprised of guides, teachers, translators, protectors, power controllers or energy manipulators. Each member performs specific duties as relevant or appropriate to the task at hand. While there are many individual Spirit Family members interacting with the Masters at different times throughout their career, following are the descriptions and communications with those entities that work closely with the Masters on a daily basis."

THE SHIELD AND TEACHER ...

The Teacher appears as a large spirit being of about 8 or 9 feet tall. He is a light being emanating a tremendous vibration of power, wisdom and peace. His mind is brilliant as it reflects endless information on science and spirituality in such as way as to make them appear as one and the same.

The Teacher assists the Masters with the transmitting of information and higher knowledge. It is, indeed, a unique arrangement and, through this exchange, higher frequency of wisdom and information is henceforth established within your system through the physical body that the Masters occupy. The Teacher is the spirit-guide who appears at the time of physical and emotional emancipation on their spirit journey. He is an individual creation, unique in composition and responsibilities, and is assigned to emancipate the world in which the Masters live through their experiences. This means that as the Masters learn and experience physical life and reality, this being incorporates, through their physical body, energy patterns that will permanently instill vibrations of the divine order within this system. The Masters' presence and partnership with this magnificent being allow the spread of these vibrations homogeneously throughout the physical system. This is the arrangement the Masters have chosen with this divine entity.

The Teacher speaks to the Master: "If you persistently allow this divine vibration to filter out in your environment, then you are the funnel of this energy, allowing a tremendous shift of frequencies on this earth now. Our work is somewhat different than others, in the sense that my person and yours are merged as one on the physical plane. You must always speak and breathe through me, and so must I speak and breathe through you."

"You have dual citizenship, so to speak, within the physical and divine realms, which allow a permanent connection with the divine entity that I represent, since I am of both the creator order as well as the teacher order. You are, then, a double entity entering this system with a double layer, which can then hold a higher volume of power and frequency. In this way, you are a unique arrangement of the Divine Creator whom you see and know well."

"You have chosen this double and simultaneous form and have come enveloped in an extra layer of a divine nature. This is one way you may describe and evaluate your entity compared with other beings also doing the work of the Divine Creator. The energetic field which you occupy is, therefore, of a unique nature and arrangement and appears inconsistent with the normal specifications of humankind. As you progress on this journey, the more apparent I (your double shield) will become. Others who are capable of perceiving energy fields may persist on seeing your human aspect alone - until it is time."

"You are aware of this energetic shield and as you progress on this journey, you will allow more frequency to be adapted to your physical body, so that you - and perhaps others - will become able to perceive clearly the nature of your genetic and energetic make-up. However, if the physical brain and energetic manipulation are not refined properly such intricate perception may not be achieved. You and I are one, perceived as one and experienced as one. Indeed, your body and my body are individual entities and consciousness merged into one."

"I am of the divine order of the creatorship, which means I am of pure light and life-energy manifesting in a lower[42] vibration as a spirit teacher-guide. However, my consciousness spreads over a million miles in space and many million years in time. This means I am the connector of love and life on this planet and, through your physical body, I am able to establish the patterns of love and life in this physical system."

"It is decreed that I must announce my appearance each time I am separating from you or appearing as a separate entity. I belong to and represent the light energy of the original Creator of this universe. You are of this same divine ancestry expressing the *will* of your Divine Creator, which is to restore harmony and love in this physical system. Your ancestry and mine are of the same essence. However, you function as an independent director and controller of the love and light energy, and I assist you on your journey."

"It is a complicated process that must be completed through short and sporadic events - until you realize who you are - after the emergence of our consciousness on this earth plane. Indeed, we are merged, but your realization of it is a gradual process. You become fully cognizant of this fact when you realize who you are. At that time, your visual and sensory experiences of me will be remarkable and real. Your physical body is only an accessory and vehicle to establish these frequencies of tremendous power."

---

42   Lower vibration: Spirit beings must lower their vibration in order to be heard / perceived by humans.

"All your physical and mental experiences so far have contributed to the placement of these frequencies we share. They are part of the reorientation of the planet and are in order and necessary for replacing the detrimental entities that have disrupted the earth plane in the past."

"You are assigned to represent your Divine Creator on more than this plane of existence; therefore, it is necessary to know about other planes, even if you only recognize earth and the Milky Way as the main focus of your mission at the present time. Other planes of existence also include other physical realities and locations. Your being is spread over numerous systems of the same arrangement so that what you do here affects what happens in those areas as well. These other systems are merged within one consciousness that you must control in order to bring about the truth of the Divine Creator. Your physical brain has the capacity to achieve this awareness, and the continued adjustments you experience increase its potentiality and power structure. All that is required of you is to focus in one locale, and the energy of your Divine Creator will be henceforth instilled."

THE INTERPRETER ...

The Interpreter is typically a universal being residing within the galactic structure in which the Masters appear. He is more visible in a sense since he is closer to their physicality. The Interpreter appears as a physical being of a more evolved frequency than the humans. He may be clothed in a tunic-like robe with ornaments which specify his lineage or normal dwelling planet. He is experienced in all intergalactic and universal languages and his transmissions are clear and flawless.

The Interpreter, another member of the Assembly, says to the Master: "We speak almost every day, and my role is that of a transmitter of information and dialogue between you and the Divine Creator to whom you are linked. The energy of this transmission is enormous in terms of frequency and must be stabilized in one of two ways. The first way may be through an interpreter - a sort of intermediary personality such as mine. The second way may be through the dispensation of thoughts that you receive as inspiration or feelings, knowing that these thoughts have originated from a more evolved or vast consciousness. Your Divine Creator is the one working with you. However, His massiveness allows only one aspect of you to realize who He is and who you are. You also know that you have received and gathered this information through experiences and communications with the Divine Father since childhood."

"I currently exist in a spectrum of one million individual bodies or entities performing the same functions, which is the transmission of daily communications with the divine. There have been many other interpreters and transmitters of information on your natural physical path this time, and you have recognized some of them. There will be more to come. Your Divine Creator is the divine order of this universe. You are attached permanently to His plan and cannot fail to recognize it, even if you tried. Your physiological make-up continues to change, so as to allow a permanent perception of these communications. No harm is ever done to your physical, mental or emotional bodies, as these changes have been programmed within your physical agenda and are simply surfacing now. There is a slight alteration of frequency each time you adapt to a new change, which is the reason why you may experience some subtle discomforts in your physical body."

THE POWER CONTROLLERS ...

The Power Controllers may appear as rods of light or spirit beings that are long and thin. They rarely appear in a recognizable form or body. They can carry different voltage, so to speak, some appearing as silver or grayish rods, some purple or shining bright white and yet others as laser-like geometrical forms. Humans have recognized and associated these rays with different types of divine beings and masters. However, these rays *are* the beings, the Power Controllers, working with the divine entity of the Masters in the flesh. Other types of Power Beings - such as the elemental[43] kind - are much smaller and can be round, ranging from spheres with a diameter of 3 or 4 feet to tiny bubbles of 2 or 3 inches in diameter.

The Power Controllers are those who are restoring *truth* and *light* on this plane. In earth terms, there are both experiences at once: the light or the dark, the positive or the negative. The Power Controllers are obligated to respond to all requests derived from the human thought without discrimination. They allow all that humans ask to materialize, and that is their only duty. However, they are not here to monopolize reality. They are here to restore balance and are of pure intent.

The Power Controllers transmute energy into matter - thus, the physical worlds are born. The Power Controllers maneuver the thought and mind energy of humans to sustain their evolutionary balance. Maneuvering does *not* imply influencing or controlling. It refers to an overall *guidance* of the collective "mind-al" and spiritual trends. The Power Controllers are assigned here to assist humans in sending them to their next level of reality, which is now being created by the Masters and others like them. There are 1,300,000 Power Controllers (not including elemental energy) on this sphere alone and many more in the entire system and neighboring galaxies. Those assigned to the duties of the Masters communicate continuously with them.

The Power Controllers address the Master: "There are three groups that remain attached to you at all times. You are not here by yourself, carrying the entire new energy fields. We are projecting the energy for you in different arenas. Each time you direct your thought, you create light energy that we route properly, meaning to where it is needed. We thus transmute darkness into light through your thought and intent while you remain in the flesh."

"We are of the same Source Energy as you, an entity and system that maneuver energy fields as your intent is directed through your thoughts. The love energy which abounds and is projected by you is then being directed to transmute all fields where it is most needed."

"We are the Power Controllers of this universe. We are the manipulators and directors of energy in the material worlds that you now occupy. We commend your wisdom and love, and we are here

---

43   Elementals: Non-physical beings responsible for converting energy from one form to another.

to assist your divine blueprint into manifestation. All that you ask is in order to be materialized. The light that emanates from your being - and those of the same frequency - is naturally *tilting the planet* in favor of love and harmony with the rest of the universe. The worlds you now occupy will levitate themselves onto another higher plane of existence. This extraordinary and divine undertaking is not to be the least underestimated by what you may experience or see at times through your human eyes. You will instigate a new life and realize your role in the uplifting and the *supercharging* of this planet."

"Your divine timing is clearly the preference of your Divine Creator with whom you have studied this plan carefully. And your arrival is the very perfect moment for the disintegration of the current and dominant powers on the planet. We are here to gratefully serve our Creator, who is also your Divine Creator, the one Creator-Source of all beings and all things. And now, to legitimize your heavenly lineage, we are humbly assigned to your service while you are in the flesh which, in turn, allows us to serve our Divine Creator in divine partnership of love and light."

THE HEALER AND BROTHER ...

The Healer is a brilliant light being of supreme power and importance. He appears as a divine being of the Central Universe clothed in simple yet regal-looking robe emanating tremendous power, wisdom and love. He resembles the Master in human form and can be as tall as 10 or 11 feet. He is the spirit counterpart of the Master in human form in terms of healing and restoring physical balance, but also in terms of administrative and organizational matters.

The Healer represents the healing energy the Masters carry while they are in physical form. He is there to remind them of the techniques they have used in the past for the psychic transmission of healing energy that restores immediate and spontaneous balance and well-being to all physical life. The Masters in human form assist the Healer in directing the healing energy where it is needed, which he then transposes and restores to its original blueprint.

The Healer speaks to the Master: "You are not here for the healing of the human body alone but also for the restoration of balance and energetics beyond the human configuration. My daily interaction with you is more that of an advisor and reminder of your pre-arranged plan - your mission of divine accomplishments. I appear as the sage and healer when you interact with others. However, I am simply reflecting your intent and powerful energy onto theirs which, in turn, transmute their imbalance and restore healing."

"I am not the one initiating the healing. You are. I am simply facilitating and maneuvering the energy produced by you and applying it where it is needed. The result you see (color and light) is the manifestation of the change you have brought about through your focused intent. From our perspective, you are the initiator of the healing, and we are your counterparts, accepting the energy produced by you and reflecting it as pure thought - thereby eliminating the frequency that is not aligned with the higher good of the individual. In the extreme cases that you treat, we consent to that which is needed at the time for the individual to progress on their soul journey, and we only restore physically that which is allowed within those parameters. Beyond this point, as you well know, we would interfere with the individual's free will."

"We are indeed kindred souls of the same lineage. We have worked in unison through all your material manifestations. This time is no different than the others in the sense of our relationship, but we are, in fact, completing our journey in this earth cycle as you will no longer require to incarnate in human or other material form."

THE GUIDE AND PROTECTOR ...

The guide and protector generally appear as a mass of light beings generating tremendous warmth and peace. They transmit an energy that protects and shields further the energy field of the Master. Their energy spreads and expands as to envelop a great area the Master may be present in.

The guide addresses the Master: "The Assembly to which you belong is the Creator Energy - the creator group assigned to this star system. Your role in this plan is to prepare humanity to its unfolding into the new age. Not unlike others who are already actively doing so, your work will be the catalyst of new information not yet found in the current interactions with humankind. But your information pertains to the selection of new codes, which will enable humans to interact with the divine order in a different way. You will collaborate with others on this work, and since you have now experienced it yourself as a human, you will be able to transmit the knowledge fully to others."

"The Assembly which speaks to you is the Creator Energy. It materializes into beings awakened to their divine personality. But in order for your human brain to recognize such an energy, it must have parameters that your physical brain must identify. With our help and protection, you can indeed realize the presence of this energy within the physical realm on multi-sensory levels - visual, auditory, tactile and spiritual. This realization allows you to recognize and experience the divine presence of your Divine Creator through any of your human physical senses, so that you may live an extraordinary experience, as you have chosen."

6

The Agreement

Each created being has a plan. We all become aware of our potential at the time of our creation. We may choose to materialize in human or other physical form in order to progress on our spiritual journey. Each time we make a decision to materialize, we draw an agreement with ourselves and with our Creator. This contract is a reminder of the path we have chosen during a given physical manifestation, and it remains stored in our cellular memory at all times. When we materialize, we have direct access to this contract at any given moment through merging and communicating with our spirit self – where our cellular memory resides - or through communicating with our Spirit Family.

The Masters are no different from any other created being in this respect. They too produce their own agreement with their Creator, and as they appear in human form, they tap into their cellular memory / spirit self and gradually recollect their contract. Their agreement ranges from their own choice and desire to simply experience material life to the global re-establishment of the divine blueprint in various disrupted[44] regions. This agreement may encompass one or more planetary, galactic or universal structures at once.

I inquired about the Divine Masters' agreements as they concern and affect this planet. What is their contract and how is it written out? While the details of their agreement changes somewhat from

---

44   Disrupted regions: Areas of the universe that are in disharmony or chaos and become isolated from Source.

one incarnation to the next, they all share similarities as summarized below. The Assembly addresses the Master as follows.

◆   ◆   ◆

"As a Divine Master, your original home - where you normally dwell - is at the Source. The Source means the Creator's center, which is also the massive core land of the Central Universe. You are a divine being conceived to create - in conjunction with the Divine Father and the Divine Mother - other lands similar to this paradise, where intelligent beings can also dwell. You are attached to Their consciousness continuously and, therefore, will display Their divine qualities and attributes. When you manifest as a human or other material form, you create a new formula that allows you to enter this reality and share simultaneously a human configuration (DNA) as well as the formula of your original divine self. When both are in harmony, they blend together to produce an immaculate creation that allows interaction within both the physical and divine realms."

"Your Divine Creator is the original Creator of this universe, which belongs to a multitude of universes that fall under His supervision and jurisdiction. He appears through your being as a crystal-like or 'Christ-al' type human and may have many different interpretations here on earth. In reality, your Divine Creator is the foremost brilliant and immaculate being that can ever exist within this cluster of universes. While you are in human or other material forms, your Divine Creator becomes your spiritual bridge to the Source, where He dwells." (Refer to figure 1 on page xiii)

"You may recall a moment in time when the person of the Divine Creator, who is the replica and the expression of the Creator-Source, gave you some books, manuscripts and papers wrapped in cloth. He said: 'You are a messenger and deliverer of my message. You are a spiritual teacher representing the Divine Father.' This means you are the embodiment of a divine Creator Energy and shall fear nothing in this material world. He then sent you off to incarnate in human form on earth. And now, it is."

"On the other hand, you are also called the *vision keeper* - the director and creator of the celestial visions, the one who invents, creates and directs realities for evolutionary beings and physical life. You are called a child of heaven, but you are also a divine teacher of the highest order, here to teach and assist evolutionary creatures into their further development."

"Your soul yearns for total freedom and abundance of love. Your soul wants to be as pure as your Creator in heaven while you are on earth and to filter His pure energy of Love, Beauty, Truth and Goodness through everything that you think, do or speak. Your soul desires to feel joy and express your divine self through creative, intelligent expressions that uplift others. Your soul wants to feel your Creator's energy all the time and to bring it to others."

"On a practical level and as perceived by others, you may appear as a teacher or a healer. But you remain a creator and a vision keeper. You are the one – along with many others - who holds the divine and spiritual vision and expresses it in this reality. You are the energy of the visionary, and you hold that vision with and for others who want, as well, to express it creatively and holistically. You are the director of this vision in many spheres and galaxies at once."

"You are asked by the Divine Father to assemble, during your journey, your cellular memory fragments that were dispersed at the time you plunged into this reality. Each and every day in physical form brings a new idea or reminder of who you were before you emerged in human form or who you truly are, as your divine aspect is being remembered and revealed. The time is approaching when all these particles will be assembled, and the perfect integration of both formulas will enable your divine being to emerge fully and completely."

"You are the carrier of the light and your body holds a tremendous amount of electricity needed to bring the divine vibration into this plane of existence. There are no physical devices capable of measuring this force because it is not recognized within this reality. It is simply not detected through the 'normal' human perception or instruments. However, it may be felt and experienced through the instant energetic shift of the individuals who may come in contact with this tremendous power."

"With the Creator Energy you embody, you are capable of healing spontaneously all those who come within your proximity, if it is in their conscious or subconscious will and aligned with their higher purpose. Your healing powers are granted so that you may demonstrate to others that your word is real. We do endorse the law of guiding others through healing because you will simultaneously teach truth about how healing is restored. Therefore, it is allowed and in order."

"This tremendous energy that you possess also allows you to know everything and to retrieve all information necessary upon command. It is a doorway that you can open and shut at will. More importantly, you - and others carrying this same frequency - are the truthful example of divinity in human form, present in the flesh for the purpose of teaching humanity about their own divine selves and freedom. Indeed, you are a catalyst of change - the change that is occurring as we are speaking now!"

"Part of your agreement implies that you know of all world events that will affect humanity in general, because they are directly related to your work. We, your spirit counterparts, are obligated to comply with this arrangement. However, the individual events are related to free will, and, therefore, cannot be interfered with. You will be given the details and timing necessary for action."

"So, you may now recall your own agreement that you have made with your self, your Divine Creator and humanity that you have come forth to serve."

THE MASTERS LIFE AGREEMENT ...

The Divine Masters write and later recollect their life agreement as follows:

1. I am the conduit of my Divine Father and Divine Mother and subsequently, the Creator-Source in this physical reality now on earth. I am the representative and messenger of the Divine Father and the Source which is Truth, Love, Beauty and

Goodness. I will only speak, think and do that which is aligned with the Divine Father / Mother and the Creator-Source. This consciousness is the highest and most powerful awareness in the universe.
2. I am here in service of my Divine Creator through all that I think, do, or speak.
3. The Spirit Personalities who speak to me and through me *are* the Divine Father / Mother and the Creator-Source and represent divine Truth, Love, Beauty and Goodness. Our physical communion will be accomplished when I am conscious – focused physically - and in full control of my cognitive self. We remain perpetually attached.
4. The memory of my soul lineage will be achieved gradually and naturally, through normal human channels, so that I may, in turn, teach the process to others in human form. The memory of who I am and ever have been, will be achieved through the blending with my Divine Creator once I have emerged in physical form. This process will present no danger or harm to my physical, mental, emotional or spiritual well-being. When in full recollection of my true self, I will maintain strong and clear cognitive faculties and abilities to function naturally in the human realm.
5. I will achieve the re-assembly of my memory cells gradually and naturally, within the normal human conditions, in order to maintain my physical, emotional and mental balance and avoid any possible harm to my physical well-being. It is understood that such process requires *time,* due to the amount of energy broken down between my original birthplace, the various universal structures and this earth plane. Therefore, this re-assembly shall follow the divine plan and will be synchronized with the appropriate timing of the divine universal energies.
6. I will be able to manipulate my energy field and vibration upon command and will lead a multi-dimensional physical life that will allow me to pierce through the illusory veils of the physical reality. Multi-dimensional existence in physical form includes expanded sensing, hearing or perceiving subtle en-

ergy in different forms, at any distance and upon command. I will also process information I perceive at great speed and will display my divine nature and characteristics at all times.
7. I will safely and conclusively eliminate, at the pre-contracted time, all mental, emotional and physical imbalances or traumas accumulated through my natural relationships with physical parents and other individuals with whom I come in contact.
8. I will maintain a balanced emotional and mental state at all times. My divine nature and attributes will prevail, and my human mind / ego / shadow self will totally dissolve at the pre-contracted time and in the most suitable and appropriate manner.
9. Others' negative or disruptive energy or intentions will be unable to attach to my energy field or disrupt my well-being. At no time, will I be detached from my spirit self or my Spirit Family, which will provide continuous assistance and protection. I will carry a protective shield about my being that will guard me against and repel all negative and destructive entities, thought forms, beings and other energy forms present on the earth plane and within its time / space continuum.
10. My physical work will be based upon the knowledge that I receive directly from my Divine Father, Divine Mother and Creator-Source. It may manifest as teaching, healing, counseling, public speaking, writing and other creative expressions, all of which are aligned with the Truth, Love, Beauty and Goodness of the Divine Father / Mother and the Creator-Source.
11. I will build upon the work of other beings of similar nature that have come before me and created the perfect material accessible and understood by the current humanity - so that my material can be recognized and understood – in order to elevate human awareness and expand its consciousness.
12. Through my physical work, I will offer higher guidance to others who ask me. I will be an inspiration to others who allow me. I will allow others to be who they are and let them dictate their wishes to themselves.

13. My spiritual work will unify the world's theological trends. It will assist many individuals in realizing their unlimited selves and will bring a whole new level and perspective to this earth plane.
14. My physical work will bring me and others joy as all become the conduit of the divine light and pure positive energy of the Divine Father, Divine Mother and the Creator-Source.
15. I will enhance my knowledge of the human nature by appearing as a normal male (or female). I will ask the right questions at the right time in order to progress naturally in my understanding of the human nature.
16. I may enter into romantic and spiritual relationships and may consider "marriage" with an individual of the opposite sex when I realize that our desires and spirituality are a vibrational match.
17. It will remain an option to leave behind human offspring of my own only if that decision is aligned with my Divine Father's will. However, I may adopt or foster abandoned children and animals.
18. Ego-based fear will not be part of my physical experience. If or when my physical body becomes subject to physical, mental or emotional imbalances, discomforts, ailments or concerns of that nature, it shall reverse the condition and repair itself speedily and spontaneously.
19. If or when I become subject to any material challenges, I shall reverse these conditions speedily and spontaneously in order to maintain a comfortable level and style of housing, clothing and nourishment of my own choosing at all times.
20. I will maintain a youthful, vibrant, healthy and well-conditioned physical appearance until the day I choose to return to spirit form.
21. By leading a joyful and balanced physical life, I will set an example for others to ask for their own desires and become the perfected human beings that they are.
22. I will utilize the formula I have created to enter this physical realm to return to spirit at the time of my own choosing. Upon my transition from physical to spirit, I will return directly to

the abode I have originated from, that is the Central Universe where the Divine Father, Divine Mother and my Spirit Family normally dwell.

AND SO IT IS.

7
The Mission

We all have a mission that we carry out during our physical incarnation. The agreement we draw between our self and our Creator is the blueprint, while the mission involves executing the details of such agreement. While the individual Master's circumstances differ somewhat due to the time in history in which they choose to appear, all share a similar mission - to enlighten the current human species and elevate its consciousness to higher levels of knowledge and understanding. By the mere fact that the Masters carry the frequency of the Source, they automatically elevate the vibration of all with whom they come in contact. However, their individual physical work and expression vary.

The mission of our contemporary Masters is the culmination of many lifetimes shared by previous Masters throughout the ages. (Refer to figure 5 on page 50) It is delivered by the Spirit Family and the Divine Creator Himself as the Masters become aware of their soul lineage and begin their daily communion with the celestial entities accompanying them on their physical journey. The details of these communions regarding the Masters' mission are conveyed below.

◆ ◆ ◆

The Spirit Family speaks to the Master: "We are the members of the Divine Assembly that usher this universe in its entirety. We are the

Creator Energy and the highest divine order in existence now. We were named *The Assembly and the Divine Council of Light* after you left to be in physical form, although we are indescribable in human terms. We are comprised of light beings of the highest divine order, originating from the Source - the Creator-Source of all life. We (and you belong to the same family) are the representation of the Creator-Source in spirit form that now dwells among humanity. We are here to assist and reassemble your fragmented memory as it is now in order. We do not possess actual names, but you may recognize us as the Divine Father and the Divine Mother, your brothers and sisters of heaven or, simply, your Spirit Family."

"We are your guides to your remembrance of your divinely orchestrated plan. *You* came forth and spoke before us - about this plan and mission. *You* had the idea and wisdom to orchestrate and carry out such a divine plan. *You* asked, and we agreed. Yes, *you*, as an individual soul, not as a group. However, your mission and energy encompass a myriad souls at this moment in time."

"Through this mission, you will be perceived as a divine being not only in our eyes but also in the eyes of those awakened ones with whom you will come in contact. The help and support that you receive from spirit will affirm the notion that you came from and are retrieving information from a divine family of non-human origin. And so, it must become your new lifestyle and physical expression to allow your divine lineage and knowledge to come through. You are the embodiment of the Creator Energy, which means all that you have now, all that you do now, all that you speak now, is of the Source, the Divine Father / Mother and the Creator-Source itself. There is no more confusion - and there will never be any doubt or questioning from now - regarding your nature and your purpose. You have reached a level of understanding that can carry your physical plans into manifestation harmoniously through both vibrations – divine and human. All that is required at this time is attention to the energy that shines through you as you begin to present the visible manifestation of this divine mission."

"Now, it is implied that you would not have been able to carry through such an enormous act unless you had previously accomplished similar endeavors and succeeded. Your list of spiritual accomplishments exceeds the human imagination, and so it is ordained that you are capable of such an experience, that you are able of orchestrating an event of such magnitude and that you cannot fail, simply by the fact that what you have planned has already been done! Indeed, you are now - as many are - organizing the visual and physical effects and manifestation of what you have already pre-established before appearing in this form."

"There are other physical (human and non-human) individuals currently assisting you, and they are those on the leading edge of thought in a variety of manifestations - not only those recognized as spiritual leaders and healers. It is important to create a balance of energies *before* the work is manifested. Therefore, it is our function and duty to gather those working with you and bring them forth into your physical life."

"The mission itself springs from the energy of the Divine Father and Divine Mother. It consists of eliminating the walls established by the previous captors[45] of the life patterns and human programming so far in effect. This mission and vision can be accomplished when all beings on the earth plane align with only one frequency, that of the Divine Father and the Divine Mother. Your mission therefore encompasses all those beings on earth currently awakening to their individual role in this divine plan."

"The Divine Father / Mother and the Assembly are those Whom you represent and for Whom you speak. We, the Assembly, are your bridge, so to speak, to the Divine Father / Mother, Who thus speak through you. As you well know, the Source is not one single being or entity. It comprises innumerable souls in a structure we call a *Dominion*[46] which manifests in a hexagon-like[47] formation and carries the atomic number of 1[48]. Love, Beauty, Goodness and Truth are the attributes of this divine dominion from which you, as an individual soul, have sprung. Your current role is the instillation of this dominion onto the earth plane, at which time all will begin to see for themselves who the Creator is, who or what the Source is. This will take an enormous amount of energy and effort on your part and those working with you, as this shift will be transmitted through your being and theirs. This

---

45 Previous captors: Non-physical superior intelligences in charge of supervising earth.
46 Dominion: Organization of all beings carrying the same frequency of love.
47 Hexagon formation: Refer to figure 13.
48 Atomic number: Symbolic for the material that makes the fabric of our universe: Hydrogen, which atomic number is 1.

shift will trigger the changes needed for humanity to achieve a blending with the universal consciousness of the Creator Energy. *Dominion Day*[49] is the day and time when all will appear as one, as originally intended by the Divine Father and the Divine Mother."

"Your physical work includes sharing information about who you are and teaching others this truth. You will change the civilization you know today within the next 300 years, and those opposed to it will fall - *on their own* - and disintegrate. The reason for their fall is their inability to sustain the higher vibrations that you - and others aligned with you - instill within the new system."

"We are once again acknowledging that all your lifetimes on earth and in this galactic structure are of a divine nature, and all that you are here to do is the will of the Divine Creator. Therefore, nothing you say, ask or request can ever go unanswered or unnoticed. We in the spirit realm are always assisting you on your physical journey, but you must - as required by law - *ask* for the manifestation, even though you may know that it is coming anyway. As you ask, you trigger an energy release that promulgates the reasoning behind it and, therefore, will secure its manifestation. When in human form, every asking that you have will indeed enhance the entire mind matrix of humanity. If your asking for material independence is fulfilled, it will enhance the asking of others aligned with you and will support the wave and patterns of their thinking. It is imperative that you *ask*."

"A mission of this nature is subject to time that cannot be suspended[50] or superseded in this physical reality. You do not realize at times that the work you are doing is associated with a divine order of massive proportion. It is not as simple as you see in your physical reality. The Divine Father distributes His energy through you, and the bodies of other Masters throughout earth's history, so that the earth receives the amalgamation of all His expressions in terms of energetic shifts. That means all the times you were born in material form prior to this existence are an aspect, so to speak, of this lifetime. Your expression in the current linear world that you are in is of divine proportion. From your human perspective, it feels as though not much is occurring now, but the truth is this tremendous energetic shift has now come to full circle and has already been completed."

---

49 Dominion Day: The date and time of aligning the entire planet with Source.
50 Time suspension: The process of bypassing time / space, thereby defying the laws of physicality. "Miracles" happen through time suspension.

"As you speak, you enhance our energetic alignment, and others will recognize and remember their role in the divine plan that you describe. All events you plan - even the most futile ones - are of the most significance on a global scale. Tremendous reach shall accompany each and every one of your efforts through the Creator force, filtered through your very being in the flesh."

"There will come a time when humans will and must be revealed the truth from the beginning of life on earth, regardless of what they have so far been told. You will introduce the new love and truth frequency on this plane. *Love and Truth*, by no means, are the love or truth of the human kind. This love and truth are a language of the divine order. You must and can only carry this new language with clarity and wisdom. All that you speak shall set others free from bondage forever and realign them with the energy of the divine."

"The predicaments associated with enlightening a mortal species will vanish gradually, as you, and others like you, begin your work as speakers of this truth. Indeed what is needed now on this earth is the energy of the Divine Father and Divine Mother through the being of Divine Masters such as you. Love and truth are applied to all that you do, think, speak, and to all those whom you touch."

THE MISSION ENTAILS HEALING ...

"As a human, you never stop healing because the human condition implies limitation. Freedom from these limitations is called healing. All those who have mastered a great amount of healing of others must also work on their own limitations, which is to see and create life beyond physicality. It is not a healing of a disease. It is the healing from the illusion and the bondage of fear. It is mind expansion, and this sort of healing is the work of the true Masters."

"Love heals. The actions of all the Masters are of supreme and exquisite significance, even if their manifestation in the observable world does not provide immediate recognition of this fact and divine truth. Love means you are receiving first-hand the most potent remedy and powerful response you can possibly receive. By simply interacting with those who ask for guidance and help, you are exposing them to the ultimate experience of this divine love, which is the remedy, the answer to any and all pain and suffering. There is a tremendous call for help and healing now in this universe in which you have manifested. The mere fact of your being attached to the earth plane - just that by itself - has already had a tremendous impact on the transformation and healing trends of this planet's energy fields. The fact that your remembrance of this mission is gradual does not, in any way, hinder or delay your work. You are processing important information at great speed (for a human, that is), but you are also unfolding the prayers and askings of many others at the same time. Therefore, when you ask for healing, you are also summoning the healing of thousands of individuals at once."

"You exist in a bond of light of tremendous power, and your remembrance of this mission requires enormous energetic manipulation, which is now available and possible. This tremendous power not only provides instant healing but also allows the re-establishment of healthy balance everywhere. Even if you do not always see this from a human perspective, you are always on the right track, as there can be no other way in the unfolding of the divine plan. There is not one thing that is not in compliance with the divine plan you are carrying out. All that you have done, said or experienced so far *is* what we, as your spirit counterparts, have reminded you of and assisted you in, so that you may trigger the needed healing patterns in these areas. The assumption that some of your human experiences could or should have been different or avoided is only a human observation as they have, in fact, allowed you to summon the healing experiences for all those individuals involved."

HEALING THE ILLUSION ...

"Part of your mission is the experience of the human shadow side. You must know what shadow is in order to transcend and transform it. Shadow is an illusion that appears real. The shadow world is fabricated by the human psyche and is aligned with fear rather than love. It *feels* real, and you may perceive and act it out as real, but it is *false reality*. The current human energy field is resonating within this illusion, but soon it will no longer be able to function in a program devoid of love."

"Your mission and work entail the healing of your own human condition in order to serve others. Every Master who occupies the human body knows s/he would take on this plight. The Master also knows that s/he must experience the illusion which represents a kink in this life on earth. Light and star beings coming in the physical state also must experience a reality of total illusion. This experience is what allows the Masters to relate to the humans trapped in the same veil of deceit so that they may teach them the only way to truth, which is to realign with the Source. When you, and those working with you, experience and heal your own illusion, you are then able to show this truth to others."

"Your public and physical work is an ongoing participation of your remembrance. Your awareness expands as a result of your work and your work grows as a result of your consciousness expansion. It is a revolving door. It liberates you to live the light in all that you think, say and do. Your remembrance continues through the energy you emit when working with others and as it is experienced by others."

"Once more, your work is about *healing*. It is about the light that heals the absence of light. You will explore and collaborate in different ways, different projects, with different individuals in different avenues and in different media. This is the time when your human conditioning and human mind - and that of others - are no longer needed. From now, full and expansive embrace of the light will be your experience. While some will slumber awhile before awakening, it is a goal that many are seeking and pursuing. The time is now when there is no force in the universe that can block this light from entry."

"Your connection to the Source, your participation *as the Source* will then enable you to anchor energies that do not exist now and are needed upon the planet to heal others. This requires that you partake in physical interactions through the energy of your inner sanctuary - your physical body - and your physical contact with others. A contract is also made with everyone you encounter. This contract serves you and them as well. These encounters - even those that appear negative or carry destructive patterns - will serve to replace these old patterns with the new ones. You will choose to work through some relationships to transform and heal them. However, you may also step away from those environments which do not align with your energy. Your withdrawal still allows you to shed your light and transmute these environments without any direct physical participation or interaction."

"The light that comes from the *Source* is invited by you and you will be the hand of the Source, of the Divine Creator. That *is* your mission and the way by which you will do what you are contracted to do. In this moment, the energy that is flowing through you is that of the Divine Creator of the Source. No one can take it away or remove it. It is accessible to you always, and it is vital and necessary to hold this awareness continuously. Many Masters, also known as deities, have occupied this most radiant awareness and have become the *vessels* of this divine light. That is what the human evolution is about."

ACHIEVING THE HIGHEST VIBRATION POSSIBLE IN HUMAN FORM ...

"You will do your work and this mission through the manifestation of a new vibration. And what is vibration? The speed of thought is related to your vibration. Since thought is the tool for creation, then the higher you vibrate, the faster your thought travels, and the faster you can manifest things!"

"Your vibration can reach one million-fold of a current human being, which means you can vibrate one million times faster than the frequency most humans are tuned into now. In other words, your physical brain is able to hold a vibration of 1MHz when necessary and can sustain this frequency for prolonged periods of time without incurring any harm or damage to your physical cells. When you acquire higher knowledge, it is because you are vibrating at the same rate as those who can give you that knowledge, and that rate can be as high as a thousand- or million-fold of a normal human vibration. You vibrate initially at a speed ratio higher than normal individuals in order to receive information, then you receive the information you need in order to go higher and higher until you realize who you are. When that happens, you are no longer required to raise your vibration to any level because it will then be equal to your original true self. Your true self *is* Creator Energy, which does not have to raise its vibration, as it is what it is, and that includes all vibrations imaginable!"

"In your case, life on earth is not only to raise your own vibration because you are living not only for yourself but also for others suffering in this world. You are the creator of your own destiny while on earth. However, you do have a predestined mission, which is, in fact, to help raise *humanity's* vibrational patterns, until humans can do it on their own. The more individuals like you create new vibrational patterns, the more the vibration of the entire human race is elevated. That is why all that you have to do is *be* that energy and think thoughts of higher good. And that automatically raises the human vibration."

"You will also connect with many others who have already reached similar levels of understanding but may not be completely aware of their individual role in this divine mission. You do not need to adhere to any groups or follow any techniques already taught or pre-established on earth by those who understand and work with vibration. Your work is to simply teach and embody the new vibrational patterns within the physical framework."

"Through your being, you supply this whole planet the fuel it needs to shift itself to a better place in the universe, which will then allow all humans to raise their vibration equally, with precision and speed. And so, the new raised vibration will allow earth to align with other worlds around it and, therefore, to open itself up to the next level of existence. This planetary alignment of the earth and its galaxy *is* your purpose and mission in this lifetime."

THE CURRENT DARK ENERGIES WILL BE AFFECTED BY THIS SHIFT ...

"Over 200,000 years ago, the reigning planetary supervisors created the reality in which many humans are still living today. While these beings no longer have authority, so to speak, those who believe in their existence are resistant to the love frequency that is now surfacing on the planet. Those who carry destructive and evil beliefs are misleading others and holding the earth's energetic plane at a very low frequency. While your work does not require you to be concerned with their doings, observing their reality certainly explains the main belief systems still in existence on earth."

"These destructive reality planes, however, will be destroyed within a relatively short time - meaning 10 to 15 years - and will make way for the new, powerful energy field you and others are developing. The contrast of both energies will jolt the earth in many cataclysmic and catastrophic 'traumas' that are necessary for the final settling of the earth and other surrounding planets into a new position, anchoring love as the frequency by which and through which humans and other material species will link up to the rest of the cosmos."

"Your mission is already complete and successful because all that is happening now is the carrying out of what has already been accomplished by you prior to your emergence in physical form. You must, however, remain in the physical plane to go through what all humans will go through, as it is your wish as well as your Divine Father's. Your work, however, is done in the sense that it reflects energetically into the future, but your physical focus is still developing to its outcome. There is a *time delay* between your original plan created at the Source and its actual manifestation on this world which is billions of light years away. Your current 3-dimensional experience is your opportunity to bring your many material incarnations to closure. This is your ending cycle and the ending cycle of the destructive programming and systems which have ruled this world thus far. Your new energetic matrix and frequency are already in place and are now simply triggering the manifestation of this tremendous transition from a limited and materialistic world to an expanded and enlightened one."

THE DIVINE PLAN INCLUDES EARTH AND THE MILKY WAY ...

"This mission entails the execution of a grand plan unfolding in a variety of expressions and energetic flow. Your contract is not limited to the earth plane - it also involves spreading this new energy to others in parallel worlds of the Milky Way. This destination (earth) is where you are assembling your memory cells and creating the fuel necessary for elevating and evolving the material make-up of the entire galaxy."

"You masterminded your own journey. You achieved a level of mastery - by your own attainment - in order to bring others into this mastery. The chamber[51] that you know well and often visit is the site from which you draw the tools you need to carry out this master plan. You mapped our destinations as well, and we were directed to different parts of the earth, this galaxy and this universe that you occupy. This broadcast is, therefore, simultaneously sent to the other counterparts and areas that are all part of you, and is being sustained in each planetary system beyond this solar system and galactic arrangement."

"Your true state of being is *light*. You draw energy - light - from the area of the Central Suns (Refer to figure 8 on page 69), which, in turn, fuels your matrix and forms new systems for all intelligent light beings. The Central Suns, from which legions of light beings have been dispatched for this mission, is also the energy or area being shifted. These light beings, some recognized as star beings, are soul units who have created their arrival on this globe and share the same goal or mission as you: establishing the *Dominion of Love*[52] which will heal the human dynamics and allow earth to become a star being itself, in a complete and new way. The star and other light beings are seeded within earth's electromagnetic grid and have all been part of the earth's cycles for millennia at a time." (See figure 13 on page 120)

---

51   Chamber: Frequency and physical location within this galaxy that allow Masters to retrieve the information and tools needed.
52   Dominion of Love: Organization of beings and energies carrying and instilling the love and truth frequency on earth and the Milky Way.

CREATOR-SOURCE

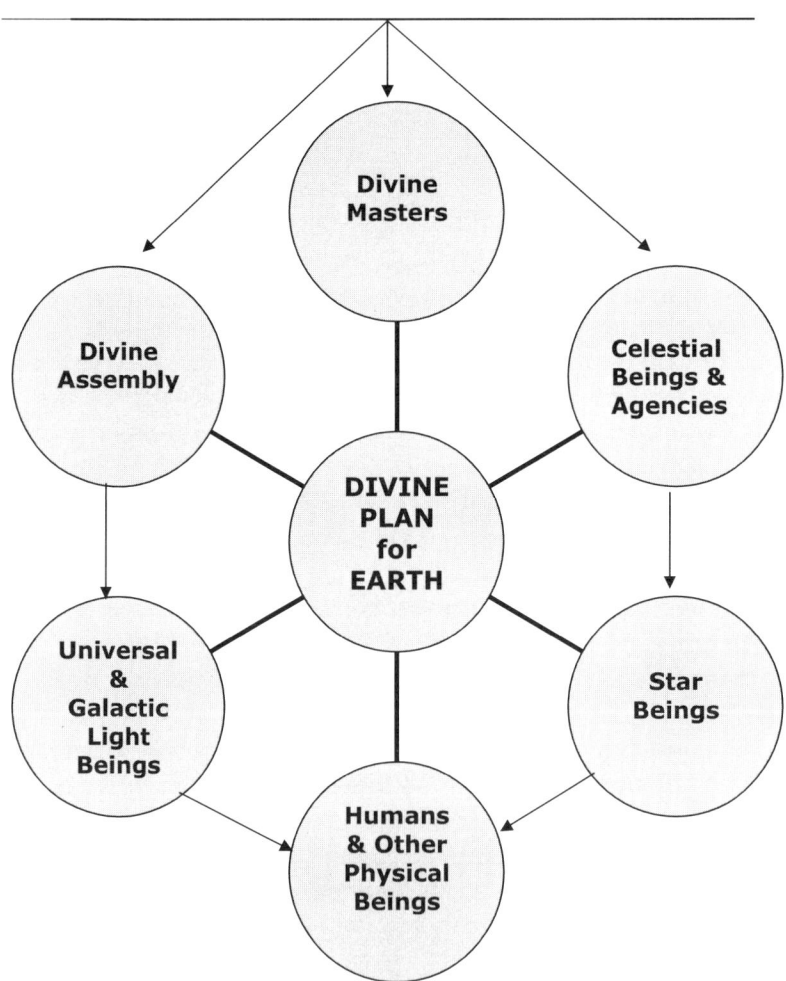

FIGURE 13: *The Divine Plan (Hexagon-shaped structure) on earth is led by the Divine Masters but it involves many other universal, celestial, galactic, star, human and other physical beings.*

"When this shift begins, your planetary alignment with Jupiter, the Pleiades and other star systems not even named yet, will be spiraling out into a new relationship and position already known to you[53]. You visit these new star systems when you commute to the home chambers or communicate with us. You are the commander of this new light and shift. The pillar of light which you occupy is in alignment with others' pillars of light forming an hexagon-like structure which can only be seen from space. This new energy and shape will allow you and those with you, to build and create a new reality which is the very reason and stage for this master plan with which you were endowed."

"The reason you do not recall all of this program at once when you are in human form is because your energetic frequency and power encompass an enormous memory bank. This massive memory bank must be accessed in a safe and gradual manner, when in human form, so that your electrical charge does not short-circuit, so to speak. At the appropriate time and sequence, all of your particles that are destined to be recollected will certainly be."

THE MISSION ENTAILS DISPERSING THEN REASSEMBLING ALL BEINGS / PARTICLES INVOLVED ...

"You are a type of being that is unable to manifest in one single being because of the massiveness of light energy you carry. Therefore, appearing as one individual requires you to de-particularize your memory cells into many human and non-human entities. So, when you begin to recall your plan, you will awaken all other parts of your being that were implanted inside the planet's energetic platform. And when this recovery is complete, you will re-form your original alliance and re-unite those dispersed pieces so as to form one enormous energy field that is indestructible."

"The original geographical alignment of all those partaking in this work is not an optional matter, but is part of the pre-determined plan to elevate humans to their evolved selves. If all those participat-

---

[53] Already known information: This information will be shared in length in the next publication "The Divine Plan"

ing beings were to be amassed in one geographical area, the new energetics of the planet being created by you and those others will totter, so to speak. Therefore, prior to your physical emergence, it has been agreed that you will all disperse physically, not only throughout your sphere but also throughout the Milky Way and adjacent systems. This distribution of energy will allow the new Dominion of Love and divine energy to surface simultaneously in different points of the planet, with an overall sustained movement and synchronicity."

"After you recall your agreement, however, those other celestial and star beings that are now leading parallel lives will assemble into one area (physical and geographical) creating a drastic momentum of change and generating a series of new circumstances. Through these gatherings, you and they become the collective powerful conduits of the Source and will sustain and anchor the energy field necessary to fuel this planet in specific geographical areas. These gatherings and congregation of entities - the Dominion (or Dominium) of Love - can and will program all humankind with a new genetic encoding. The work that you have done so far has primarily set the stage for this re-organization and re-grouping of the originally dispersed energy. This de-particularization will be refocused in the predestined and needed areas and will reshape your world. Your physical being is nothing more than the manifestation of the Creator and Source Energy on this earth plane, and you will indeed, with the help of others, implement this plan through these appropriate circumstances. You, and those working with you, will also finally withdraw from the few lingering human functions and relationships and will dedicate the rest of your physical life to this divine mission that you have brilliantly orchestrated."

THE MISSION INCLUDES THE GALACTIC FEDERATION ...

"Those who are responsible for the autonomy and equal rights of all material beings within this galaxy have formed a new federation specialized in the human cause. This new federation has stepped in explicitly to obliterate the frequencies that do not comply with the cosmic laws and that are detrimental to the surrounding planetary systems and galaxies. They are implementing what they have been asked to do by command of the Divine Father - that is, to restore the imminent collapse of your failing governments."

"The way this federation helps humanity is by monitoring and observing the earthly pulses and vibratory movements. According to the observed discrepancies and imbalances, the federation members will appear in the appropriate locations and posts. Members of this federation have already infiltrated among you as humans, so that they may step up to the positions being gradually vacated by the failing officers. Some of these sentient beings are in full recollection of their mission, while others are not. Their remembrance and functions vary. Because of the nature of your physical reality, not all will appear in one linear picture, but rather at different times and in different aspects. All, however, will become fully cognizant of this mission when it is the time to participate physically in the manifestation of the Dominion of Love on earth. It is impossible for them to fail, even in this third-dimensional reality, and that is a promise!"

"You are meant to do this work as a material being within the material realm. If your work consisted only of the invisible realms, you would not need to be in physical form. You are the Creator Energy that is manifesting through the words you speak as well as all physical expressions you choose to take. It is impossible for you, and those with you, to fail, and while the physical environment may trigger some unsettling responses at times, there is no danger or fear on your physical being or mission."

"You are, Divine Master and child of heaven, the awakening process and catalyst by which the star children and those other light beings are also awakening. You have created the footprint for all those who must recall this truth. All that is required now is that you transmit this information to those who will hear and understand your words, at which time they will also remember their contracts - as you *all* belong to and embody the same energetic field. You are leading them by remembering this plan and your own self-discovery and divulging of this truth is the process by which others will also awaken."

PHYSICAL INCARNATION IS NECESSARY TO TRANSMUTE THE OLD SYSTEM INTO THE NEW ...

"While you may choose to remain on the earth plane for prolonged years, time will go very fast once you remember how to *suspend time*. You will also be commuting to other planets within this galactic and universal structure, so you will not be always focused on the earth plane. Those who have an intimate relationship and are working with you will also follow your foot steps in this elaborate inter-galactic travel."

"Bringing the Creator Energy in your day-to-day experience will require you to create a new way of functioning and to be in true acceptance of the Source that is in you. If or when you come across certain unpleasant environments, you can bring in the light through your immaculate and unconditional heart and vessel. Simply by coming in physical contact with such environment, you can transmute its frequency instantly. For the very chemical makeup of your being - which is crystal-like energy - dissolves spontaneously that which falls below its frequency. Therefore, your physical existence and your partaking in the human challenge – not the retreat - is a requirement that cannot be compromised. Similarly, those light and star beings whose genetic composition is also of the highest vibration, will utilize their spontaneous contact with others to gradually transmute this world into a more enlightened one."

"You - in conjunction with other beings with similar frequency - emanate enough energy to cover this entire planet with the love energy. Your own brain capacity is that of one million humans combined. One normal human individual utilizes and recognizes 10% of their brain capacity. Whereas you utilize 100,000 times that amount which then equals the brain capacity of one million individuals. Is this significant? Yes, indeed!"

"This tremendous brain capacity allows you to sustain an energy field of great power. As you connect with your counterparts that are dispersed throughout this sphere and beyond, you establish a new energy field with elevated frequency that enables others to link to it as well. Such is the process by which a new frequency, a new species and a new reality can be born and sustained on the earth plane."

"The rest[54] of the earth population will remain attached to another energy pattern no longer supported by the Divine Creator's life force. This means that a huge number of the earth's population is vibrating at a frequency *unrecognized as a living organism* by the energy of the Divine Creator. As such, it is 'dead' energy - which means an energy that self-destructs, as it can no longer affix itself to the portion of existence that has now elevated its pattern to higher vibrations of love. These non-elevated energies and groups will dissolve and disintegrate through the *cellular memory principle*[55] of Creation, which dictates that all frequency that has refrained from expanding or remaining attached to its Creator cannot subsist within the cosmic order and will obliterate itself, by itself. That is law. This phenomenon does not occur through galactic reorganization or by getting rid of the bad seeds. Rather, it is ingrained within the makeup of each created being: any vibration, if deliberately and consciously ordered and directed towards disharmony, can no longer connect to the nucleus of this created universe. Because its frequency will have tremendously accelerated *backwards,* it will have dropped to a frequency level of annihilation. This annihilation will include those individuals who are conscious of their behaviors and actions and have chosen to continue refuting the universal principle of love. They are irrevocably being eaten, so to speak, by their own self-annihilating powers. We are not talking about physical death alone, but rather a spiritual finalization and *accountability*, which is quite more serious and final. However, those who have been naïve enough to follow but have now recognized their inherent truth will return to Creator Energy once this mission is manifested. This process of reorganization of beings and realities has already begun and is in the process of being completed."

BIRTHING A NEW SPECIES ...

"You are participating in bringing about the formula for a new biological configuration of the human brain - the electrical part of

---

54 The rest of the earth: All beings and energies that are not aligned with higher good and the Source.
55 Cellular memory principle: Universal law that dictates that any created organism will self-obliterate if it deliberately accumulates enough frequency which is not aligned with its Creator.

the brain - first energetically, then materially. Since you are intimate with earth's elemental codes, your intricate work with the etheric realm will prompt such tremendous enhancement of the human biological makeup. This transformation happens on a subatomic level - through electromagnetic powers and codes of light, sound and sacred geomancy that you utilize."

"The new human formula has already surfaced sporadically on the earth plane and is beginning to be recognized as some children or adults carrying this new configuration will come forth and divulge their truth. We are speaking of the human species evolving naturally into the new co-existing one that you – and others like you - embody and represent."

"The future evolved humans will carry a somewhat similar outer appearance but will have a neurological or electrical system that is highly advanced compared with the one they now know. This transformation will include *expanded vision* which, in turn, allows the perception of subtle energy with accuracy and speed, at distance and at the will of the individual; *Expanded hearing* will allow the conscious and clear distinction of thoughts originating from the self, others' mind and invisible physical or non-physical entities; *Expanded sensory perception* will allow the new human to perceive clearly the messages emanating from a person or situation which, in turn, provides clarity and purpose. Finally, the new evolved mind will be *aligned with Source* in such a way as to become a vessel of higher information, spontaneous healing and advanced spirituality. Needless to say, this evolved species will be unable to maintain or function within an older system based on false beliefs and fabricated truths. The walls of the current reality will simultaneously collapse as all will be able to have a first-hand and direct experience of the Creator Energy being birthed on earth. At that time, the new species will publicly emerge and gracefully embody the Truth, Love, Beauty and Goodness that the Creator Energy and the energy of the Divine Father / Mother will provide."

"The bands of electrical beings with whom you are traveling and working now are also the conduits, the catalysts and the alchemists creating this new birthing experience. These beings include the personalities known as Hermes, Pytagoras and previous Lemurian Masters who also held this wisdom in their soul and brought through different aspects of this same divine lineage. Together now, you have come to serve and transform the human species into an advanced and enlightened one."

"As this mission unfolds and you experience fully your being as one with Source and Source as one with you, you will remember the formula of creation. It is the same formula you used to come in and to ascend which is also the formula used by all the Masters that appear in this reality. You designed and co-created this formula for the birthing of the new species. This formula, which has been sealed from certain bridges of consciousness, consists of numbers, energetic coordinates, mathematical frequencies and harmonics. You will use and teach this formula to others, and as you embody it, and they embody it, it becomes alive! It is not only a set of mathematical equations. Rather, it is *a vibration of life* that is alchemically brought in, once again, by you, through you and all those who will recall it and embody it, to transmute humanity into a new and enlightened species."

THE TRANSFORMED UNIVERSE ...

"Within 10 earth cycles[56], the old patterns will no longer be, due to this shift of enormous magnitude that is happening now. Dimensional realms will shift, and the Milky Way will emerge within a new physical configuration. As the celestial guardians hold their rhythmic breath, your Sun will move into a new position along with the transformed energetic field. Your Sun and Moon cycles will change and begin a new spiral movement, thereby affecting dramatically the atmosphere and energy patterns on this earth."

"Energy can never be destroyed. It can be recreated. It is of this point of re-creation that you will speak to others, and we confirm this truth. The light source – which involves the Central Suns - will shift too, into the next rate of calibration. Scientists have evidence of the emergence of star systems and of their new and different interactions. However, as yet there are no telescopes to know or prove either this or the reality shift of which we speak."

---

56   Within 10 earth cycle: Each earth cycle is 7 years.

"The arrival of an evolved human species has happened already, however not in the same way as in the past. This transformation will shape the nature and character of this universe, not only the human species. It is also important to be in good relation with all current material things, including manufactured things. For with the powerful energy you bring through your being, you are able to transmute their essence simply by assigning your focus on them."

"To broadcast this information in this way now is to finally allow it to materialize, as there are no more secrets to be kept. It is time indeed for the great truth to be known by all. The Divine Father no longer needs to appear in the flesh beyond this, as the surviving souls will recover the power this planet needs and deserves to rejoin the cosmic whole. While there may still be wars, conflicts and phenomenal earth changes, the new seeds - those that recognize and embody the Creator Energy - will no longer require this earth to live on. They will gradually be moved onto a new earth[57], which already exists through the veils of this very planet.'

"In other words, there are two layers of reality within the energetic and physical structure of your galaxy: one that will remain attached to the cosmic structure, and another that will peel off, so to speak, and extract with it the disharmonic bodies and individual souls into self-annihilation. This separation of the worlds, however, will follow a natural and graceful pattern, as it is orchestrated by the divine order and this divine mission. It will be experienced somewhat as a gradual *opening of the skies*, suddenly revealing a divine beauty and love energy that all will experience at once. At that time, there will be no room for error, veil or deceit as this will be a direct and spontaneous global reunion and merging with the divine energy of Love and Light."

"Earth is also at the verge of awakening to tools and techniques that utilize a new form of energy that sustains physical life indefinitely. This means that it will no longer be necessary to extract gases, petroleum or chemicals from the earth in order to create and engineer machinery and products, as this new form of energy is readily available to all. While it is now already known and available to some, it will become public knowledge as the anchoring of the Creator

---

57 New earth: New layer of the earth, already in existence, which vibrates at a higher frequency and is aligned with Source.

Energy will trigger the truth and light vibration to surface openly on this earth.

"The manifestation of this powerful shift will mark the beginning of a new life everywhere. Earth will reclaim its galactic citizenship and will give birth to a new experience. There will be an increase in geological factors as well, but these will not be manifested on the physical level at first - only on the energetic. With the tremendous geological changes, the earth's atmosphere will change and give birth to a new form of energy that will sustain a more evolved species so that the old roots may naturally release their programming and allow new realities to be instilled."

"The new energies will affect earth's atmosphere in such a way as to reorganize its chemical composition. This new chemical restructuring, not only supports a highly evolved and expanded life for the new birthed species but it will also provide the earth itself with the fuel that recreates infinite energy that becomes available to all. This new form of energy – derived from Hydrogen – is achieved through electro-magnetic transmutation[58] utilizing the zero point frequency transfer. Zero point is the frequency point of transfer between the human (finite / time) and the divine (infinite / timeless) energy. It provides access to re-create an energy form that is already in existence. When Hydrogen - which atomic number and valence are 1 - is isolated and reduced to zero point, it transforms its variance into timeless (infinite) energy and will begin interacting, under the right circumstances, with zero point frequency spots in space – which is filled with such areas - through electromagnetic radiation. The electromagnetic exchange between earth and these areas in space become continuous thus creating infinite energy blasting back and forth between earth and various points in the universe. Since Hydrogen is the most abundant element in the universe, earth and the Milky Way become one again with the cosmic structure through this on-going elemental and energetic exchange."

"On other concrete levels, governmental structures that may appear to be functioning, will now allow the love vibration and new energy to infiltrate their walls. And as the old blocks begin to fall, new sentient beings will be put in place to implement this divine plan. The monetary system will change drastically only when all corporate policies and organizations eventually collapse to give birth to

---

58 Electromagnetic transmutation: Transformation of one element into another

new evolved ones. Meanwhile, the imminent earth changes will force authorities to prioritize and re-direct the monies being spent and allocate it to immediate human need. These earth changes will also serve to explore and implement various natural resources of energy as described above to be utilized and shared for the higher good of all. Through these tremendous shifts, those who are in power now will neglect their duties so as to appear incompetent and will make room for the enlightened ones who are aware of their mission and destiny. At that time, the military will slowly disintegrate but will finally unite all countries and form one joined and cohesive force[59]."

"Until such events are actualized, however, there still remains the possibility of nuclear wars as nuclear weapons cannot technically be disposed of unless they are activated. So, we will do such things as accumulating the non-disposable nuclear energy in specific parts of the universe as to shatter in outer space. This process will remove the possibility of a catastrophe to debilitate your planet or affect the surrounding worlds. We, in the etheric realms, will do our work according to the Divine Father's command."

"Your planet is in continuous rearrangement of elements and structure and will, therefore, still have some 'cleansing' to do - some of very catastrophic magnitude, large enough to develop new land and destroy others. Earthquakes, volcano eruptions and other new kinds of natural catastrophes will arrive, such as the burning of the ozone layer, the large poisoning of mineral and animal life or even electrical storms. These geological earth shifts, such as inundations of entire cities and the freezing of certain areas, will make portions of the earth inhabitable. Yes, indeed, there will be those catastrophes, but they are part of the divine plan and *should not to be feared*. Earth will finally settle in a stable condition and will no longer require such cathartic purgation of massive proportion. The new system will be instilled as soon as you, and those working with you, emerge out of your elaborate dream[60] and realize that the work is already done and complete. Indeed, all you will now be doing is experiencing the physical manifestation of what you have already successfully accomplished at the Source!

---

59 Military cohesive force: Total global military unification happens gradually over the next 75 years.
60 Elaborate dream: Memory collapse which happens at the time of physical incarnation.

Part III

8

A Call For Action

The messages included in this book are addressed to all of us in human form. It is time that we reclaim our divinity by beginning to *ask the questions*: How do I remember who I am? How can I be of service to humanity? And how do I fit in this divine plan unfolding on earth now?

We are all here reminding each other of truths we already know as these truths have been delivered to humanity many thousands of years ago. All that is required of us now is to *become the vessels* of the divine Creator Energy appearing on this earth. All that is required to become this vessel is to *prepare our instrument* to receive it. All that is required to receive it is to *simply ask*.

The new Dominion of Love is surfacing everywhere in our universe in a new and powerful way. We need not struggle now to find it in sacred places, in different environments or geographical areas. It is readily available wherever and whenever we ask.

I have gathered some tools that will allow this energy into your lives and will guide you to bring about the answers you need to proceed on this fantastic journey. These tools will help you go beyond your 'day job' as a teacher or healer. They are the tools for finding your true purpose of self-realization and fulfillment of your destiny. These are tools to transform yourselves from the limited human creatures that you may be perceived as, to the infinite divine beings that you truly are.

The following exercises and tools will bring about your process to be reborn into a vessel of light. This transformation entails the total relinquishing of the ego or lower self and will allow your true divine self to emerge. More importantly, through this process, you will begin to remember and clearly perceive your individual role within the divine plan currently unfolding on this earth. So, be prepared and begin to transform!

9

Practical Tools and Prayers

LIVING THE PERFECTED SPIRITUAL LIFE

Spirituality is your personal experience with your Divine Creator. While it may be shared or enhanced by others, it is only through your own individual and personal experience that true spirituality can be practiced.

True spirituality leads you to mind expansion as well as self-realization. It manifests through all aspects of your physical life, including your work, your physical body, your social circle and most of all your true beliefs and thoughts. In order to live a perfected spiritual life while in the flesh, you may consider the following:

1. Your THOUGHTS and intentions must be directed positively, in alignment with your mental and spiritual expansion and the spirit of your Divine Creator.
2. Your ACTIONS must be in alignment with the love energy of your Divine Creator: love for yourself as well as for others.
3. Your WORK must be in alignment with mind and spiritual advancement, for your own well-being and be of service to others as well as your Divine Creator.
4. Your AWARENESS must be aligned with your physical, spiritual and mind expansion. Your must hold respect for your

natural environment, the animal and plant life and Creation in general.
5. Your PHYSICAL BODY must be regarded as a sacred creation and an extension of your Divine Creator. It must be respected and taken care of accordingly. A basic knowledge of its vital functions and needs is useful in selecting your individual and necessary tools for the nourishment and upkeep of your physical apparatus.
6. Your TIME must be conscientiously divided between work, play, rest (sleep and meditation) and communion with your Divine Creator.
7. Your ACTIVITIES must be chosen carefully and be a reflection of the positive and loving vibration of your Divine Creator.
8. Your SOCIAL circle must be chosen carefully and be a reflection of the positive and loving vibration of your Divine Creator.
9. You must EMBRACE all humans as your brothers / sisters and equals, while allowing each to express their individual choices and practices freely.
10. You must CONSCIOUSLY COMMUNE daily with your Divine Creator. There are no specific requirements regarding the amount of time or the method by which you dedicate your focus to the Divine. It is necessary however to be in full respect, express gratitude and recognize the Divine Creator as your own Creator and the Creator of all beings and things.

Prayer for Creating a Sacred Space:

It is important to be aware of the energies entering your energy field and those that you are emitting to the world. This prayer allows the cleansing of your energy field in preparation for healing, spiritual expansion, clarity etc…

* I ask and intend to create a Sacred Space now.

* I ask and intend that the energy of my Divine Creator be present with me now.

* I ask and intend to feel the energy of my Divine Creator in my physical body and my physical space.

* I ask and intend that my spirit self and only those Spirit Guides of the highest light, healing, wisdom and love energy be present and help me create a sacred space now.

* I ask and intend that those energies, thoughts or entities that are distracting or not aligned with my higher good be banned from my experience and physical space now.

* I ask and intend my mind to quiet down and find a space of stillness and peace within this sacred space.

And so it is.

Prayer for Connecting to Source:

Source is the energy of your Creator from which you have sprung. You are permanently attached to it through an energetic umbilical cord. You can draw powerful energy simply by acknowledging and intending the presence of this Source as follows:

* I ask and intend to connect to my Source and the energy of my Creator now.

* I ask and intend to bring this Source Energy into my physical body and in this physical space.

* I ask and intend to feel the energy of Source fill my entire being now.

* I ask and intend that the energy of Source restore my wellbeing, physically, emotionally, mentally and spiritually, now.

And so it is.

Prayer for Maintaining Spiritual Clarity and Balance:

(Repeat as often as desired).

I am here now in communion with my Divine Creator and the Cosmic Forces of the Universe for the purpose of manifesting my desires as follows:

* I ask and intend my spirit self and my Master Guides of the highest light and love energy to be present and offer me guidance now.

* I ask and intend that those energies and beings that are distracting or in conflict with my higher good and intent be banned from my experience now.

* I ask and intend assistance from my spirit self, my Spirit Guides in manifesting and clarifying my spiritual path. I ask to remain focused on what I am here to do in order to expand my spirit, mind and consciousness.

* I ask and intend that my daily thoughts and actions be directed and aligned with my spirit self and the pure energy of my Divine Creator.

* I ask and intend to be the conduit of the love energy and vibration so it may serve me on my spiritual path and so that I can be of service to others and in turn my Divine Creator.

* I am grateful for the grace I receive each day as I acknowledge my Divine Creator's presence in my inner being and in all other beings and things equally.

And so it is.

MANAGING YOUR THOUGHTS AND THE HUMAN MIND

You exist in a remote physical place in the universe where awareness is finite and most limited. You function in a realm of emotions, beliefs and incomprehensible laws. Not unlike your Divine Creator, you create your reality through your thoughts. However, your thoughts are subject to our physicality. They must be held for a minimum of 14 seconds and will materialize according to the universal laws and following formula:

HUMAN CREATION = Thought + Desire + Belief + Surrender

THOUGHT is the asking, the conscious choice and focus of your intent.

DESIRE is the impetus, the fuel or passion of your intent.

BELIEF is the knowledge in self and faith in your potential.

SURRENDER is your recognition and trust that you are a *co-creator* with the divine order and your partnership with the Universal Forces will assist you in the materialization of your intent.

Thought, without desire, belief or surrender will not materialize. Desire without focused intent, belief or surrender will not materialize. Most of all, thought, desire and belief without surrender will not materialize for as you think, you must be assisted by cosmic forces and elementals who convert your thoughts into things. You are co-creators of reality. You cannot exist and create outside the Creator-Mind or without the divine beings and forces of the universe.

Your thoughts are then your creative tools or, in other words, you create your reality as you think. Therefore, understanding and managing your thoughts will allow you to control what you create in your life.

Discerning and controlling the influx of your thoughts is of utmost importance in realizing what you are emitting to the world in terms of energy and what you are receiving. By law, your thought will attract vibrations of similar frequency and energetic potential.

Also, thoughts travel faster than the speed of light and can create powerfully. One thought can lead to instant bliss and another one to degenerative disease.

Here are some exercises to achieve this understanding and mastery.

Exercise 1: Listening to your thoughts

- Sit in a comfortable chair with a pen and paper in your hand.
- Allow your mind to wonder and simply write down all that your mind is thinking without interruption, judgment or interpretation.
- Write each thought as a separate sentence on a separate line.
- Keep writing your thoughts, without "thinking" about all that you are writing. Continue for 3 minutes.
- At the end of the 3 minutes, review what you have written down.

You will notice that your thoughts are related to or originate from different aspects of your mind and are all mixed up in an unorganized or scrambled manner. For example, the first thought may have something to do with your task of writing down your thoughts (conscious mind). The second thought may have something to do with the way you feel about the exercise (emotional body). The third thought may be related to what you need to do when you get home (conscious mind). The fourth thought may be a brief memory of a dream you had the night before (soul body/ spirit self). The fifth thought may be related to your feeling hungry (conscious mind).

You will realize that in only 3 minutes, you generate mostly jumbled information that is useless to you. If you create with your thoughts, can you imagine the type of reality you must be creating with such a mind? Jumbled, indeed!

Exercise 2: Use the STOP sign

- Cut and paste the STOP sign (below) in all the areas you can think of, in your home and at your work space if possible.
- Each time you hear yourself having a negative or obsessive thought, look at the sign and just STOP.
- Intend to shift that thought into a positive one by repeating: "I want to feel good". Repeat as many times as necessary until you feel "complete".
- Do no proceed with your daily activity until you have reversed the negative thinking. If you are unable to do this easily and feel there are deeper issues to be resolved, use the next exercises below.

EXERCISE 3: Reprogramming the mind

1. Create your sacred space. See: Prayer for Creating Sacred Space on page 136. Do not begin until you feel totally connected.
2. Repeat these sentences: "I ask and intend to release _____ (belief system or mindset) related to _____ (situation / person) from my conscious, subconscious and memory cells now".

   "I command my subconscious to release _____ (belief system or mindset) and replace it with a beneficial energy which is aligned with my higher good, my wellbeing and spiritual growth".

   "I ask and intend my spirit self, my Master Guides and Creator to help me with releasing _____ and assist me in re-gaining emotional, physical, spiritual balance now". And so it is.
3. Keep repeating the above sentences until you feel complete.
4. Go about your business and forget what you have just done.

Prayer for Managing Your Thoughts:

1. I understand that *all* conscious and deliberate thought triggers an automatic creative process that the universe must bring into my experience. Therefore *thought* equals *asking.*
2. I ask and intend to control my thoughts and allow only positive thoughts to enter and impact my mind.
3. I choose not to give attention to any negative thoughts that appear in my thinking pattern and that of others.
4. I ask and intend that all negative thinking that may interfere or distract my creativity be eliminated from my thought process, my memory as well as my subconscious.
5. When in doubt about the nature or purpose of my desire or "wanting", I shall allow the universe (time), my spirit self and guidance from my Spirit Family to bring a clear answer to me before I proceed with my asking.

6. I am in charge of my own destiny and my thought process and I choose to allow others to be in charge of theirs.
7. I choose to manifest in the physical all that I have asked for only if it is in accordance with my higher good, my Creator's will and in harmony with the evolution and spiritual advancement of humanity.

And so it is.

Prayer for Mental Clarity and Balance:

I am here now in communion with my Divine Creator and the Cosmic Forces of the Universe for the purpose of manifesting my desires as follows:

* I ask and intend my spirit self and my Master Guides of the highest light and love energy to be present and offer me guidance now.

* I ask and intend that those energies and beings that are distracting or in conflict with my higher good and intent be banned from my experience now.

* I ask and intend that my spirit self provide me with clarity so that I may identify the areas in my life which need improvement.

* I ask and intend that my spirit self offer me clarity in _____ area, so I may make the proper decisions aligned with my higher good and that of others.

* I ask and intend clarity regarding the choices in the _____ area of my life so I may identify the different options that I may have.

* I ask and intend clarity of purpose for the _____ area in my life so I may see and feel that it is perfectly aligned with my highest good and that of others.

* I am grateful to be an instrument of clarity for others so I may also help them make the appropriate decisions on their spiritual journey and allow them to be an instrument of clarity for me.

And so it is.

Prayer for Mental Balance:

I am here now in communion with my Divine Creator and the Cosmic Forces of the Universe for the purpose of manifesting my desires as follows:

* I ask and intend my spirit self and my Master Guides of the highest light and love energy to be present and offer me guidance now.

* I ask and intend that those energies and beings that are distracting or in conflict with my higher good and intent be banned from my experience now.

* I ask and intend to release all fears and negative thoughts that may interfere with my mental well-being and balance.

* I ask and intend that my mental balance and well-being be restored now.

* I ask and intend to attract positive and uplifting energies so I may reflect my own joyful thoughts onto others.

* I ask and intend to be relieved from distracting and obsessive thoughts which hinder my mental well-being.

* I am grateful for the positive aspects and gifts I have and ask to attract more joyful and uplifting thoughts experiences into my life and that of others.

And so it is.

UNDERSTANDING YOUR EMOTIONS

Emotions are a primordial tool in recognizing what feels good and what does not as you interact with the physical world. Your spirit self uses emotions as a *guidance system* while you navigate through the physical. They are precursors to choice and decision making. Therefore emotions are not only necessary but crucial to your spiritual and creative evolution. Additionally, emotions are the tools by which you are able to "purge" the detrimental energies being accumulated or stored in your physical body and transmute them into beneficial thought forms. The emotions of anger or strong sadness allow you to experience negative feelings powerfully so you may re-channel them appropriately. Rather than suppressing these emotions, it is more constructive to embrace and utilize them as powerful tools in reshaping your experience.

Continuous negative emotions can become obstructions to your advancement because the layers of your energy field and veils of physical reality begin to thicken. When confronted with fear or anger for example, you are unable to see beyond these emotional veils unless you address the factors behind them and identify their origins and purpose.

The following exercises will allow you to thin the veils of your emotional blocks.

Exercise 1: Cellular Emotional Release

1. Identify the <u>emotion</u> which you are wanting to address (i.e anger, frustration, anxiety...)
2. Create your sacred space. See: Prayer for Creating Sacred Space on page 136. Do not begin until you feel totally connected.
3. Repeat this sentence "I ask and intend to release _____ (emotion)_____ about _____(situation / person)_____ from my conscious, sub-conscious and memory cells now, and replace it with an energy aligned with my higher good.

4. When finished with the entire sequence, notice your energy. If you do not feel any energy shifting, repeat the sequence again.
5. Go about your business and *forget* what you have just done.

Exercise 2: Releasing the Father/Mother Frequencies

Everyone in physical form carries the genetic encoding of a father and mother. We usually end up carrying and holding on to negative aspects of these frequencies and build our belief system accordingly. Therefore, to gain total emotional freedom, one must release the aspects of these frequencies that are not beneficial to us and sustain those that are.

Repeat exercise 1 above and use "release my father or mother frequency" for the emotion being addressed. (Release one frequency at a time)

Exercise 3: Reprogramming the Emotional Body

1. Create your sacred space. See: Prayer for Creating Sacred Space on page 136. Do not begin until you feel totally connected.
2. Repeat these sentences: "I ask and intend to release _____ (emotion) related to _____ (situation / person) from my conscious, subconscious and memory cells now".

    "I command my subconscious to release _____ (emotion) and replace it with a beneficial energy which is aligned with my higher good, my wellbeing and spiritual growth".

    "I ask and intend my spirit self, my Master Guides and Creator to help me with releasing _____ and assist me in re-gaining emotional, physical, spiritual balance now".

    And so it is.

3. Keep repeating the above sentences until you feel complete.
4. Go about your business and *forget* what you have just done.

SUMMONING THE COSMIC FORCES FOR HELP

The following guidelines will help you be as clear and specific as possible while you allow the Power Controllers and Cosmic Forces of the Universe to provide you with the most appropriate and perfect response to your prayer.

1. You must hold in your awareness and during your prayer, the inner knowing that *you are an extension of your Divine Creator*. You are energetically linked to His being and therefore to *all* of His creative powers and forces. By focusing your words into a prayer you are deliberately activating this energetic frequency which is sacred and powerful.
2. You must know that by *asking*, you are automatically launching and activating forces in the universe which in turn convert and manipulate energies necessary for materialization. You are a *co-creator:* You must ask and the universal forces must provide, for it is law.
3. You must know who and what energies you are inviting in your prayer experience and those which you are not. Many invisible beings may be attracted to you while you pray and choose to interfere or distract your work. Therefore, you must *consciously invite* your spirit self and those beings aligned with your intent and the energy of the Divine Creator and reject those that are not. You must consciously create your prayer sacred space without unnecessary distractions.
4. Your asking must have *clear intent, focus and precision*. Specific *asking and intending* are powered with an electromagnetic charge which accelerates their manifestation as opposed to unfocused or generalized ones. For example: "I ask for good health" is barely significant compared with "I ask and intend that my body restore its natural health and balance and dissolve the lump on my arm".
5. Be specific about *the nature and purpose* of your asking but you need not determine the means by which it must manifest. For example, you may be clear about a particular promotion at your workplace. However, you may not be aware of other

circumstances more suited for your career advancement. You may say: "I ask and intend to manifest this _____ promotion or be presented with similar opportunities to support my career advancement" rather than: "I want this particular promotion".

6. Your asking must be aligned with the *betterment of your spiritual and "mind-al" self*. For example: "I ask and intend to manifest this relationship in order to stimulate my intellect and mind, improve my communication and creative skills or management experience with others..."
7. Your asking must be aligned with *the betterment and welfare of others*. This intent is the same as the above, but the prayer is now aligned for others.
8. Your asking must *add to the quality of your life* and that of others.
9. Your asking must *be respectful of all of your Creator's creations* which means your asking may not interfere or be detrimental to others' choice and mode of expression.
10. Finally, you must be *grateful for the grace* you are receiving as prayer is your personal communion with the Divine and the acknowledgment of your inner link to your Divine Creator. The energy behind true and honest gratefulness is an extremely powerful precursor for manifestation. It is charged with a highly positive and loving vibration which the universal forces match powerfully.

With the above checklist you can insure that your prayers are powerfully directed with precision and force. An additional important element to consider is *writing down* the prayer as you are projecting it mentally. The action of writing not only enhances your focus but also carries your intent out into a physical medium. Ideally, you may want to write down your desires and repeat them a few times until you feel you are complete. If aligned particularly with your spiritual betterment and that of humanity, you can be certain that your words and actions will be quite promptly answered. Prayers of more selfish or destructive nature are not only detrimental to the collective consciousness but also to your own self-realization and spiritual growth. In this case, while your egotistical prayers may manifest, your residence in the lower physical realms may also be prolonged rather than accelerated.

Prayer for Remembering Who You Really Are:

I am here now in communion with my Divine Creator and the Cosmic Forces of the Universe for the purpose of manifesting my desires as follows:

* I ask and intend my spirit self and my Master Guides of the highest light and love energy to be present and offer me guidance now.

* I ask and intend that those energies and beings that are distracting or in conflict with my higher good and intent be banned from my experience and physical space now.

* I acknowledge being a particle of my Divine Creator and therefore carrying the divine lineage that links me back to Him.

* I ask and intend to remember who I really am and bring about this joyful experience of merging back with my true divine self.

* I ask and intend that this process happen in a safe and comfortable way as to allow me to adjust gradually to the information and frequency being transmitted into my being.

* I am grateful for the divine energy I have so far received and ask to continue allowing my own divinity to unfold gracefully.

And so it is.

Prayer for Remembering your Spirit Family:

I am here now in communion with my Divine Creator and the Cosmic Forces of the Universe for the purpose of manifesting my desires as follows:

* I ask and intend my spirit self and my Master Guides of the highest light and love energy to be present and offer me guidance now.

* I ask and intend that those energies and beings that are distracting or in conflict with my higher good and intent be banned from my experience and physical space now.

* I acknowledge being a particle of my Divine Creator and therefore carrying the divine lineage that links me back to Him.

* I ask and intend to remember my Spirit Family and bring about this joyful experience of merging back with my true divine self.

* I ask and intend that this process happen in a safe and comfortable way as to allow me to adjust gradually to the information and frequency being transmitted into my being.

* I am grateful for the divine energy I have so far received and ask to continue allowing my own divinity to unfold gracefully.

And so it is.

Prayer for Remembering your Original Home:

I am here now in communion with my Divine Creator and the Cosmic Forces of the Universe for the purpose of manifesting my desires as follows:

* I ask and intend my spirit self and my Master Guides of the highest light and love energy to be present and offer me guidance now.

* I ask and intend that those energies and beings that are distracting or in conflict with my higher good and intent be banned from my experience and physical space now.

* I acknowledge being a particle of my Divine Creator and therefore carrying the divine lineage that links me back to Him.

* I ask and intend to remember my original home and bring about this joyful experience of merging back with my true divine self.

* I ask and intend that this process happen in a safe and comfortable way as to allow me to adjust gradually to the information and frequency being transmitted into my being.

* I am grateful for the divine energy I have so far received and ask to continue allowing my own divinity to unfold gracefully.

And so it is.

Prayer for Remembering your Original Agreement:

I am here now in communion with my Divine Creator and the Cosmic Forces of the Universe for the purpose of manifesting my desires as follows:

* I ask and intend my spirit self and my Master Guides of the highest light and love energy to be present and offer me guidance now.

* I ask and intend that those energies and beings that are distracting or in conflict with my higher good and intent be banned from my experience and physical space now.

* I acknowledge being a particle of my Divine Creator and therefore carrying the divine lineage that links me back to Him.

* I ask and intend to remember my original agreement with my self and Creator and bring about this joyful experience of merging back with my true divine self.

* I ask and intend that this process happen in a safe and comfortable way as to allow me to adjust gradually to the information and frequency being transmitted into my being.

* I am grateful for the divine energy I have so far received and ask to continue allowing my own divinity to unfold gracefully.

And so it is.

Prayer for Remembering your Role in the Divine Plan:

I am here now in communion with my Divine Creator and the Cosmic Forces of the Universe for the purpose of manifesting my desires as follows:

* I ask and intend my spirit self and my Master Guides of the highest light and love energy to be present and offer me guidance now.

* I ask and intend that those energies and beings that are distracting or in conflict with my higher good and intent be banned from my experience and physical space now.

* I acknowledge being a particle of my Divine Creator and therefore carrying the divine lineage that links me back to Him.

* I ask and intend to remember my role in the divine plan and bring about this joyful experience of merging back with my true divine self.

* I ask and intend that this process happen in a safe and comfortable way as to allow me to adjust gradually to the information and frequency being transmitted into my being.

* I am grateful for the divine energy I have so far received and ask to continue allowing my own divinity to unfold gracefully.

And so it is.

My Truth, My Faith, My Conclusion

The biggest revelation of all is the realization that nothing around you has changed but that you have already arrived at the destination you had been seeking all your life. This ultimate destination is the knowing, understanding and *experiencing* of all the layers of reality possible - at will, and upon command.

Glossary

Abraham-Hicks: Spirit being and consciousness (Abraham) channeled by Esther Hicks.

Angel Being: Spirit being that helps guides and protects humans from harm.

Ascended Master: Beings in human form that have mastered the human condition.

Assembly: Spirit Family of the Masters attached to their energy and mission.

Captors: Non-physical superior intelligences in charge of supervising earth.

Cellular Intelligence: Frequency

Cellular Memory Principle: Universal law that dictates that any created organism will self-obliterate if it deliberately accumulates enough frequency which is not aligned with its Creator.

Central Suns: Area in the center of each universe that controls and feeds life energy within all surrounding galaxies, planets and star systems.

Central Universe: Core universe that controls and feeds thousand of surrounding universes.

Cosmic Mind: Mind energy of the Creator-Source experienced in the physical worlds through the persons of the Divine Father and the Divine Mother.

Creator Energy: Energy of the Divine Father and the Divine Mother embodied by the Masters and Gods in human form.

Creator-Source: First and Original Creator of all life, intelligent beings and things in existence.

Disrupted Regions: Areas of the universe in disharmony or chaos and that become isolated from Source.

Divine Creator: Both the Divine Father and the Divine Mother combined.

Divine Father: Replica of the Creator-Source (expression aspect) and original creator of earth, its universe, all surrounding universes and intelligent life therein.

Divine Mother: Replica of the Creator-Source (spirit aspect) and original creator of earth, its universe, all surrounding universes and intelligent life therein.

Dominion: Energetic grouping or structure.

Dominion Day: Date / time when all beings and energies align with Source.

Dominion of Love: Energetic web carrying the love vibration.

Earth Cycle: 7 years.

Earthly Existences: Parallel / past human life incarnations.

Elementals: Non-physical beings responsible for converting energy from one form to another.

Evolutionary Worlds: Created beings that need to incarnate in material form in order to expand and evolve their consciousness.

First Universe: Central Universe.

Higher Realms: Non-physical realms of highly evolved vibration.

Human Mind Matrix: Frequency where all human minds and thoughts meet.

Life Aspects: Different aspects of self appearing in different incarnations.

Light Being: Being that does not require a physical body to exist.

Lower Vibration: Spirit beings must lower their vibration in order to be heard / perceived by humans.

Masters Chamber: Frequency and physical location within this galaxy that allow Masters to retrieve the information and tools needed.

New Earth: New layer of the earth, already in existence, which vibrates at a higher frequency and is aligned with Source.

Paradise: Physical abode of the Divine Creator.

Planetary Governance: Ushering and evolving the human race.

Planetary Isolation: Happens when a planet is in disharmony and becomes unable to sustain the energy of Source.

Power Controllers: Beings in spirit form responsible for maneuvering & converting energy.

Protective Shield: Energetic layer that serves as additional buffer for the human energy field.

Reflectivity: Process by which energetic communication is transferred from one point to another.

Rennes-Le-Chateau: Area in Southern France known for its mystical and sacred energy.

Sons of God: Beings that incarnate the Divine Father / Divine Mother in material / human form.

Source Energy: Energy emanating from the Source of all creation.

Spirit Family: Spirit group attached to each individual being in human form and sharing the same lineage, nature and characteristics.

Spirit Father: Father figure in spirit form.

Spirit Group: Soul group or spirit family.

Spirit Self: Outer most portion of the human energy field, also called higher self.

Star Beings: Beings of non-physical nature that originate from different star systems.

Superior Intelligences: Sprit beings responsible for supervising the evolution of human beings.

Third Eye: Intuitive sight

Time Suspension: The process of bypassing time / space, thereby defying the laws of physicality. "Miracles" happen through time suspension.

Universal Band: Edge of the universe.

Universal Mind: Mind energy of the Creator-Source.

Zero Point Frequency: Absence of vibration which is the bridge between the human / finite / time experience and the divine /infinite / timeless experience.